NIGHTWATCH
AND DAYSHIFT

POEMS — 2007-2014

BY WILLIAM IRWIN THOMPSON

Published by Tree of Life Books
102 Sandy Ridge-Mt Airy Road
Stockton, NJ 08559
www.treeoflifetreeofjoy.com

Publisher's Cataloging-In-Publication Data
Thompson, William Irwin
  Nightwatch and Dayshift

ISBN: 978-0-9839188-9-9

1. Literature. 2. Poetry. 3. Lindisfarne Association.
4.William Irwin Thompson.

Printed in the United States of America

Second Edition

NIGHTWATCH AND DAYSHIFT

POEMS — 2007-2014

BY WILLIAM IRWIN THOMPSON

Tree
of Life
Books

BOOKS BY
WILLIAM IRWIN THOMPSON

*The Imagination of an Insurrection: Dublin, Easter 1916:
A Study of an Ideological Movement, 1967*

At the Edge of History: Speculations on the Transformation of Culture

Passages about Earth: An Exploration of the New Planetary Culture

Evil and World Order

Darkness and Scattered Light

*The Time Falling Bodies Take to Light:
Mythology, Sexuality and the Origins of Culture*

*Blue Jade from the Morning Star:
An Essay and a Cycle of Poems on Quetzalcoatl*

Pacific Shift

Gaia, A Way of Knowing (editor)

Selected Poems, 1959-1980

Imaginary Landscape: Making Worlds of Myth and Science

Gaia Two: Emergence, The New Science of Becoming

Islands Out of Time: A Memoir of the Last Days of Atlantis: A Novel

*The American Replacement of Nature: The Everyday Acts
and Outrageous Evolution of Economic Life*

Worlds Interpenetrating and Apart: Collected Poems, 1959-1995

Coming into Being: Artifacts and Texts in the Evolution of Consciousness

Self and Society: Studies in the Evolution of Culture

A Diary of Sorts and Streets, Poems

Still Travels: Three Long Poems

*Culture Evolution of the Sense of the Sacred
from Shamanism to Post-Religious Spirituality*

TABLE OF CONTENTS

BOOK ONE: NIGHTWATCH

1. Vade Mecum Angelon 12
2. Voyaging Alone Together, 1972 32
3. Nightwatch 34
4. My Bedroom Window 36
5. The Pleiades 38
6. The Trinity and My English Club Chair 39
7. Cardiovascular Rehab 44
8. Hokusai's Great Wave 46
9. After Heart Surgery 47
10. My New Titanium Valve 48
11. My Medicines 49
12. Mysticism and Science 50
13. The Dragonfly and the Hummingbird 52
14. Back Story 53
15. Herrn Walter Benjamin: Mosca, Colorado 55
16. A Dialogue of Self and Daimon 56
17. The Jester's Marginalia 58
18. Iona 62
19. A Pagan Ur-Text of the *Lebor Gebála Érenn* 64
20. Slipping on Ice 74
21. The Pink Conch 76
22. Meditation on a Roman Mural at Pompey 78
23. *Sunt lacimae rerum et mentem mentalia tangunt* ... 80
24. Joined Bodies, Separated Minds, Summer 1976 ... 81
25. *Das Ewig-Weibliche zieht uns hinan* 83
26. The Facts of Life 85

27. Medical Records 87

28. The Death of Neda 89

29. Playing around with Sonnets 90

30. Question to Extremeophiles 91

31. The Hand 92

32. Bolides and Volcanoes 93

33. The New Age Cult of 2012 94

34. Nature 95

35. The Ant 96

36. A Dandelion 97

37. Choir Boys 98

38. Surfing the Web 99

39. Category Mistakes are Poetry in the Making................. 100

40. *Monono* Aware 101

41. A Matter of Scale 102

42. The End 103

43. Emily at Amherst... 105

44. Quantum Entanglement... 106

45. *La Escritura del Dios* 108

46. Bedtime Story for Androids... 109

47. To the Israelis and the Palestinians................................ 110

48. Digital Government: Homage to George Orwell,
     Philip K. Dick, and Wendell Berry 111

49. Urschrei... 113

50. Cézanne 114

51. An Apology to Kenneth Rexroth 115

52. Remembering a Night with Stockhausen 118

53. After Closing Blues.. 119

54. 3:00AM Blues 121

55. A Lazy Summer Afternoon 123
56. Pantoum 125
57. The Dark Winter Afternoons in Portland 126
58. It's Time 128
59. Retired 129
60. Beatrice, Summer 1977 130
61. For Beatrice, October, 2013 131

BOOK TWO: A PORTLAND CALENDAR

1. "Welcome to Maine" 134
2. On Moving to Maine and Reading Two
   Anthologies of New England Poetry 135
3. Chapter Seven 137
4. Amigos 138
5. Longfellow Square 139
6. Munjoy Hill 140
7. The Seagull 141
8. October 142
9. Congress Street, November 143
10. In Gritty McDuff's Pub 144
11. Lunch at DiMillo's Floating Restaurant 145
12. An Economy of Scale 146
13. At the End of the Ferry Pier 147
14. March Streets 148
15. March Rain 149
16. St. Cuthbert's Day 150
17. Middle Street 151
18. The American Economy 153
19. Congress Street, April 154

20. Hurricane Bill.. 155
21. Casco Bay.. 156
22. Carleton Street Haiku.. 158
23. Maine Mall... 159
24. In RiRa's Irish Pub, I... 161
25. In RiRa's Irish Pub, II.. 163
26. Pencil Sketch.. 164
27. In RiRa's Irish Pub with Horace's Second Ode................ 165
28. Pub Poem to Horace's Fifth Ode in Gritty McDuff's........ 167
29. Pub Poem: To Horace Eleventh Ode by Way of Hafez........ 168
30. To Horace's Ode XIII 169
31. Pub Poem To Horace, Liber II, XI 171
32. Pub Poem in Bull Feeney's to Horace, Book III, Ode XVI......... 173
33. After Catullus II 175
34. After Catullus XXXII.. 176
35. After Catullus 51, which itself is after Sappho 128 177
36. After Catullus LXXXV 178
37. Free Street... 179
38. Back Cove.. 180
39. Another Kind of Madeleine....................................... 181
40. The Conference of Crows... 182
41. Mid-Winter Mood... 183
42. Winter Haiku... 184
43. Icicles.. 185
44. Maine Landscape.. 186
45. The Modern Poet.. 187
46. Nancy Grayson's Bookstore...................................... 188
47. Seasonal Change... 191
48. Radiators 192

49. The Striking Sound of Raindrops.................................... 194
50. Gerontion... 196
51. Clytaemestra... 198
52. On Reading *The Penguin Book of English Verse*
    on my iPad and Exercise Bike 199
53. Apartment Living.. 202
54. Leni Riefenstahl and the Triumph of the Super Bowl................. 204
55. The Nineteen-Fifties 205
56. Longfellow Square... 206
57. An Urban Anchorite.. 208
58. The Western Promenade 209
59. Coffee Cantata: *Die Unerträgliche Sehnsucht* 210
60. Poetry.. 211
61. Neuroscience I.. 212
62. Neuroscience II 213
63. Reincarnation and the Akashic Record 214
64. Lindisfarne Fellows Conference, 2011 215
65. Zuccotti Square, 10/31/2011 216
66. Extraordinary Rendition.. 217
67. Blue Moon, August 31, 2012 219
68. Anataman.. 220
69. Philip K. Dick Speaks from Beyond 221
70. Smartphones... 222
71. Coming out of the ER in Damariscotta................................ 224
72. The Western Promenade: Instructions to My Daughter
    for My Last Rights.. 226

BOOK ONE

NIGHTWATCH

VADE MECUM ANGELON

Proem: Anima Mundi

On Earth we never got higher
than Machu Pichu, lower than
that cataract of the Blue Nile,

unless you count your recesses
Grand Canyons of God as I did,
your hostile eyes Everest heights.

Now that there is nowhere to go,
we stare apart at the same sea.
When we traded one another

for partners in slow caravans
we knew it was for good, that we
could go no further in bodies

that had drained themselves of secrets
inscripted in red and white
parchments a god had torn in half.

I hear you still recalling me
as you stare at that cold ocean,
not Indian or Pacific.

Know that I have already passed
into the angel I mistook
you for and am alive in her

about to start the last voyage
we once began but could not end,
mistaking one for another.

The First Lesson

1.

First the stellar cloud
in butterfly folds
of blue, gold, magenta—
a double torus rotation
of a perfect hypersphere.

2.

I understood this to be
the colorful plasma
from which you stirred,
alert to the clay wet
fingers of dark matter
that shaped you
from the radiant death
of exhausted stars.

3.

Then a Saturn ring
around a fast
rotating neutron star
that in its orbit
hummed two notes
of decreasing pitch
as the longer
elliptical wing
swung round—

a ballet dancer's
Fouetté en tournant,
or an angel
with extended wings.
Was this your history—
the Pleiades' lost star—
or our common ancestry
and former clouds of glory?

4.

Carboniferous ferns
compressed to coal,
I burn and run
on millions of years
of animal sex
compressed
to pistoned heat
in an iron age.
What am I
paired to you?

The Second Lesson

1.

At seventy,
it is not morbid
to think of death,
anymore than it is
to dream of birth
inside the womb.

2.

The body registers
the aftershock
when you're alone
in someone else
you cannot see
but can conjure
and configure
with other organs
of perception—
not sight exactly,
vision certainly.
The spine becomes
the axis of a torus,
body's other architecture,
its three dimensions.
doubled by spiraled wings.

3.

At death it's all
upside down again,
the sky a sea above
as you swim up
into a second sky
where sight is not
so object bound
but a fluid medium.

4.

The body is embedded
in realms of desire
that got us here,
voyeurs of lovers
who parented us.
The bed takes the stamp
of curving forms,
valleys we stream into,
caught by sexual dreams.

5.

At first the angel
takes the form
of loved wives,
then madder loves;
you replay the moves
and parts of love,
but the body

starts to break up—
pixels of thought—
thighs become clouds,
the vulva apart
in golden light
of sky not bed.

                6.

If you do not
follow her up
into abundance
but linger attached
to the parts, she returns
in a swirl of cloud
that becomes her face,
smiling and saying:
"I keep losing you."
If you follow her,
she lifts you up
from going down
on her in folds
that shift to clouds,
then a stellar cloud
of gold, red, magenta,
and intense sapphire blue.

7.

How did they know
to call Marlene Dietrich
Der Blaue Engel,
whose wide full
Brünhildic thighs
invite being born?

8.

Conscious birth,
conscious death,
if you hold on,
attached to the old body,
the delta becomes mud,
the piss and shit
and rotting brain
of old age caught
in hospitals
and nursing homes,
bound in tubes
and drugged in order
to keep angels out.

9.

Why do I always go back
to where I have been,
seeking to repeat
the vision of last night?
Each night is new.
If I seek to go
to hypnagogic states,
she'll hold me
to the waking mind,
showing it's closer
to spirit than soul,
as air is to light,
and water is to mud.

10.

Awake, "now" becomes,
not successive thoughts
backed up by the beat,
but the spaces between
heartbeat and thought—
the background mind
on which thoughts float,
surface waves on a sea.

11.

Held in Indra's jeweled net
of sapphire stars,
I see in the opening
of the third eye,
she 's keeping me
from the astral world
of indulgent desire,
revealing I am
actually in her,
as I was once
inside the womb.

12.

What others will see
as the body's death
will actually be
me coming not going.

13.

To be born you leave
the womb in a birth
that is like being blown
along the entire shaft
of your finally extended body.

14.

Inside this angel's body
of 3-sphered light,
I learn that I too
have her stellar form,
and that my life has
more than its years.

15.

In reversing time,
you become your parents
before you were conceived,
then realize they're symbols
and you end
in your Daimon
with your Angel
becoming one again.

The Third Lesson

1.

In hypnagogic trance
of lucid dream,
you conjure a woman
built out of pure
desire—the one
you never had;
but now you've got her–
her thighs around you,
breasts against your chest,
her wet lower lips
anointed in pure lust.
You look into her eyes
and realize
she's an automaton,
little better than a coin
operated blow job
or a blown-up plastic doll.

2.

So how long
do you wish
to linger here?
Your angel watches,
above the hypnagogic
tranced erection.

She has more time
than you have,
better learn
how to spin
the flax of sex
into the linen
of your own
light shroud.

The Fourth Lesson

1.

The trick is to recall
the other life refracted
in image garbled dreams,
to see virtual worlds
equally playing us.
In lucid dreams we make
the plot up as we go,
then wake to find that life's
another laptop game
in which we've cast ourselves.

2.

Earth's our avatar,
a resource colony,
with old empires
serving as metaphors
of star systems
with stark archetypes
of opposing minds--
Orion's Egyptian
hierarchies versus
light Pleiadean love.
Science fiction acted out
what we could not recall.

3.

I am the director
and the lead as well
and must be the two
at once, recovering
the mind I had before
I was born for the part.

4.

If I walk off the set,
thinking the director
all important, I fail
to see the star needs me
to be in human time--

the two supporting roles
of wise man and good friend
require that I have
the mind of director
and lead at once: two birds
on the selfsame tree, one
watches, the other tastes
the red ripening fruit.

5.

After the Earth is cleared
and Adam becomes clay
again at the bottom
of a reabundant sea,
these chimeric starlings
will be the new creatures
of Heaven on Earth
in New Jerusalem's
green and pleasant land.

The Fifth Lesson

1.

I can see them now,
in my mind's eye
can envision
the point ahead.
Marked by the spear
of Celtic Lugh,
the Solstice path,
they are moving
to the still point
where we converge.
I have become
my own Stonehenge
timed sacrifice.

2.

I face the South,
daimon to West,
angel to East,
and await
the Pleiades;
my time-bound I
will vanish once
all consummate
their light bodies
of storied earth

and neutron star
over the crossing stone.

3.

On Iona,
I through Brigid's
forehead star
saw the sacred
gold trifoil knot.
Now three become
one in the point.
I find myself
increasingly
needing to be
in conscious death
daimon and angel
at the end of me.

The Sixth Lesson

1.

Often I would see them
in vatic dreams—
daughter and mother,
and would know
who they were—
Tara and Quan Yin,
Persephone and Demeter,
the entwined Goddess
of Maid and Mother—
of Ain Ghazal
and Çatal Hüyük.

2.

In Gobekli Tepe,
in Çatal Hüyük,
Malta, Newgrange,
Stonehenge
and the hill of Tara,
the year's king
must die.
The Great Mother
alone endures.
She is not fat,
or fertility fetish;
she is vast,

containing everything.
An icon of time,
her lunar womb
is the wound that heals.
It is the phallus
that rises and falls,
vanishing with its
poignant time.

3.

For most my life,
I have pursued
the daughter
as Tara or Shakti,
intent on Tantric
erotic transfiguration
to bodily escape
Holy Mother Church,
or just my Catholic Mom.

4.

In Tiahuanaco,
the Island of the Sun,
and the night shore
of that vast Andean lake
under unknown

constellations,
I lived all that out——
shuddering in her
in the tantric union
of the red and the white.

                    5.

Now it is again
the Mother's time,
in death as it was
once in birth.
The yoga shifts
from sight to sound,
from the third eye
to the crown:
the infant's fontanelle
comes out first,
the yogi's crown,
re-enters first—
the prow in the cleft
of parting waves.

6.

So it is time
I face again
the primal cleft
dividing worlds
in a new Tantra
where the red
and the white
are in the spine—
as taught
in that ancient
Tibetan art
of dying alive.

VOYAGING ALONE TOGETHER, 1972

...tanto magis ille fatigat
os rabidum, fera cordo domans, fingitque premendo.

Standing in silence in front of Luxor's
Winter Palace and staring at the Nile,
a man in a gray kaftan and turban
approached us, and bowing modestly
he gestured with mute hand, offering us
a ride at sunset in his faluka.
I looked at the simple wooden vessel
with its tall mast and single sail, the sun
about to set, and agreed without fear.
You sat forward to port, and alone. I
stood by the mast, not bound to it with ears
closed because your Venus body said "Come!"
while your Artemis eyes always said "Go!"
The full moon rose over the horizon
and you looked out over the wide Nile,
recalling other nights, other lovers,
unable to be in that beautiful
moment sailing in the full moon with me.

Accepting my solitude, I looked up
at the mast and watched it pitch back and forth
between different stars and knew I had
done that before in another life.
Sailing from Alexandria to Crete,

lying flat with my head touching the mast,
I had watched that finger point to the stars
as I wondered, Platonist that I was,
when I would return to my native star.

We never spoke, the faluka turned round
and we sailed back to the Winter Palace.
That night in our large room with high ceiling
and twin beds with their doubled solitudes,
I watched you set your pen and dream notebook
on your side table, preparing yourself
for a virgin's intercourse with a god.

In my bed with my hands under my head
I looked up at the ceiling that blocked out
the stars and wondered why I had chosen
to travel alone with a raped sibyl
through ancient and archetypal landscapes
that summoned the old gods to sleep with her
and forced me to watch my obstructed lust.

NIGHTWATCH

1. 4:00 AM

I am up it is the night that goes down
on whoever is outside cold exposed
to stars that have their way with you even
when you are not looking for transcendence
they can take you over like a woman
addicted to the liquored taste of men
whose skill stuns and undoes embodiment
in its opposed alchemical excess
but I am inside and alone under
a roof that is insensitive to stars
at an age when illness is prophetic
and unveiled angels become more real
than a whipped and foaming sibyl ridden
to frenzy by a lost god caught on her.

2. Alchemy

Midnight trance induced sun and moon nerves hold
physiologies of transformation
poteen testes distilling alembic
whiskey's occult aquavit boiling still
into an upended brain while the pipe
that leaked in another's red flooded cunt
withdraws to the occult go fuck yourself

androgyne groin where the clitoral glans
stares at seductive dakini visions
as one more than any other surrounds
me with her enantiotropic thighs
and encloses us under her light veil
insulating the etheric body
from other women you mistook for her.

3 Yoga Nidra

Driving back to body's waking mind
in her top down Lincoln convertible
her blond and light easy flirtatiousness
makes me forget the dream's lucidity
and the old fairy tale rules that I must ask
her name otherwise she will appear time
and time again in play's many guises
maid and mother movie stars and lovers
but instead I ask her which she prefers
William or Bill as if either one were
were really who I am as I become
less than I was to suggest that she drive
us back to her place and not to where we're
heading down the exit ramp waking up.

MY BEDROOM WINDOW

I find my Portland apartment
bedroom window is like Stonehenge,
autumnally aligned to frame
the rising of the Pleiades.
This just seems to happen to me.
They follow me around, looking
out for me in case I forgot
myself in the low horizons
of Manhattan and Cambridge streets.
The first time I saw their rising
was on Iona in Traigh Bhan,
the retreat house owned by Findhorn
at the north of the island where
Vikings were said to have slaughtered
monks, leaving blood on the white sands.
Evan was with me, home-schooled
that fall about Stonehenge, lay lines,
old cosmologies, Celtic lore,
and all the Seventies unearthed
from Tolkien to Alan Garner.
Our beds in the upper story
of that Scots-cold drafty house were
level with the windows, so we
could lie flat and look out over
the red rocks of Mull from the green
ancient marbles of Iona—
sea-washed oval stones we'd gathered

from St. Martin's cave at low tide.
Then like an Annunciation,
the Pleiades rose in the East
over the horizon of Mull.

That time I did not hear the stars'
high pitched music awakening me
at midnight in the tower at
Crestone, to see in the skylight
the Pleiades above my bed.
Now in Portland as an old man,
I am comforted my windows
are perfectly aligned to them
so that I can watch their rising
to their zenith above my roof.
I hope one night I will join them,
finding the yogic way to die,
going out through the Celtic tonsured
skylight at the top of my head.

THE PLEIADES

Why, more than any other stars,
do the Pleiades call to me?
Not all the ancient Egyptian
lore of Orion's Belt, nor the
cosmic stream of the Milky Way,
not even all the electric
lit up windows of Manhattan
seen by tantric lovers aloft
on doomed Atlantean towers
can haunt me like the Pleiades.
They call me out of my known self—
the names and thoughts attached to me—
and I see with another eye
a densely compressed neutron star
with an unequal oval ring
humming two notes as it rotates
with these wounded angelic wings.
Was there a death of the seventh
star that orphaned a race of us
and sent our exiled souls to Earth?
I long to return, but then fear
that our star died to propel us
into human birth and that Frost
was right that Earth is the right place
for love, as I am here not there.

THE TRINITY AND
MY ENGLISH CLUB CHAIR

1.

In the Newgrange triple spiral—
given a spin by Saint Patrick
into the Christian green shamrock—
pagan mysteries are turned out
and the Triple Goddess erased,
replaced with a bland meaningless
pigeon, war god Jahveh, his son
who was obedient and meek
and awfully good at dying.
Christians could not escape the facts
of life and the Goddess sprang back
as Mary, enduring female
who holds the dead male in her arms
in the new form of Mother Church,
as you see in the Vatican,
polished up by Buonarroti.
A prehistoric mystery
is embodied here, one you can
find in icons and rituals
of the neolithic Near East--
Gobekli Tepe's phallic head,
or Catalhuyuk's wall paintings--
great female space and short male time.

Listening to the Ninth Quartet
as an adolescent I felt
the opening of the third eye,
the spinal rush upward of light
that dissolved the room into space
with infinite stars and two eyes,
beautiful and terrifying,

behind the canopy of space
that looked through me as I, shaken
by the joy of return, screamed Yes!
to everything, cancer and All.
I took this vision to be Christ—
the Cosmic Christ not just Jesus
who lived in him for the three years
from the Jordan baptism by John
to the Crucifixion when he
cried out at his abandonment.
It came in the year I was not
in school or at work in the course
of life, but apart, turning
my cancer into liminal
states suspended between two worlds.

II.

Fifty years later in Cambridge,
in meditation in a chair,
I floated out of my body,

or became aware that I had
a body above the club chair
as I drifted down into form.
For an instant between two worlds,
I floated in the space of stars,
hearing the music of the spheres--
each existent being sounding
out its melodic signature
in a state of cognitive bliss.
I knew this to be God as All--
Great Mother and Matrix in one.
Here too I was outside the course
of life and recovering from
open heart surgery, and out
the world in a liminal state.
First thyroid cancer, then the heart.

III.

God the Father appeared at last
four years later, again in a
condition of kidney collapse,
dehydration, high altitude,
and too many antacids of
calcium carbonate that brought
me into hypercalcemic
delirium right as I was
meditating all through the night
in practice of yoga nidra.

I was two minds, dream and waking,
so I cannot prove my visions
that visionary night were not
failed kidneys and toxic dreams.
It seemed I surfed the edge of dreams,
delirium and waking mind,
using illness shamanicly,
the way shamans will use their pain,
or lack of water, lack of sleep,
knowing as I traveled I was
still sitting in my grey club chair.
I flew above an island reef
at the edge of a sphere of light.
The angelic beings danced in
mudras of six wings and not limbs,
for they were rooted to the spot
like aspen trees to a clear stream.
I landed and saw the dawn rise.
This sun became a hypersphere,
and I was granted permission

by the Seraphim to go in.
I entered and felt exalted
in joy and bliss beyond belief.
When I came out I was flying
back to a great ringed waterfall.
David Spangler appeared by me,
remarking: "Now that was something!

As if for a Daimon this was
no common mystical vision.
I looked down the high waterfall
and realized it led straight down
into the lower hardened worlds
of brute matter and burning time.
Then we jumped like Butch Cassidy
and the Sundance Kid. The Daimon
disappeared and I made my way
alone through all the places I
had lived, ending in awareness
of the comfort of my club chair
in a Zen cabin in Crestone
that could no longer be my home.
Illness now lay claim to my life
and I would be transported to
Alamosa and Santa Fe,
and finally to Portland, Maine
and another bout of open heart
surgery with metallic valve.
I do not know why I am here,
since twenty books are quite enough,

and I no longer feel the need
to be smart in public and make
my books a commercial product.
So I sit, meditate, and wait
in my soft gray English club chair.

CARDIOVASCULAR REHAB

Astride my fixed exercise bike,
going nowhere particular
in space, looking for more pulsed time,
my prostrate perineum hurts
from the narrow leather seat crammed
into the crack of my sad ass.
I read poetic collections
on an ipad because I'm bored
with churning butter out of air.

Poetry began in Sumer
as worksongs sung for the goddess
Inanna and her young lover,
the humble shepherd Dumuzi.
At the edge of the cluttered town,
on opposite sides of the road,
the girls churned the thickening butter
as if they were jacking off boys
to turn their white cream to butter
to cook up with their new laid eggs.
On their side, the girls would sing
antiphonal of Inanna:
"Who will plow my vulva?" and laugh
while the boys, on the other side,
milking their goats would stroke their teats
as if they were their own stiff cocks
squirting semen into the girls'
clay bowls of thick curds and thin whey.

Then the boys would answer the girls:
"Dumuzii will plow your vulva!"
And the girls giggled, as girls do,
and life was fun and needed no
exercise to keep it alive.

HOKUSAI'S GREAT WAVE

Each year an illness demands something more
for me to exchange from my heart's ribbed cage.
Like Rilke's panther pacing out his grave,
I stare at a blank barred infinity.

In old age each year is a fractaled age,
a curled wavelet hanging from the wave,
as the great wave itself hangs from the sea,
both dependent on the moon's gravity.

As wave and wavelet hit a fractaled shore,
the coast also shows self similarity,
as do mountain waves like snow-topped Fuji.

These iterating patterns include me.

So I give up one thing and another,
drawing to that point heart will uncover.

AFTER HEART SURGERY

The two note call of the loon sounds
across the cardiac lake.
I walk the corridor alone.
It is neither night nor dawn.

I find my name
inscribed on monitors
fixed to the wall.
A wave passes through
echoing the call
of the other loon
on the fog-lifted shore.

MY NEW TITANIUM VALVE

My mitral valve,
clanking away metallically,
sings of the Titans
titanically.

The primordial stream
of blood wants to clot—
how much time, Doc, have I got?

So coumadin
is the fix I'm in.
Thus do I survive—
acutely chemically alive.

MY MEDICINES

Hydrochlorothiazide
brings the Old Irish poems
of heptasyllabic verse
to mind in trochaic art.
"I and Pangur Ban my cat,
tis a like task we are at."
Metoprolol Tartrate and
Warfarin Sodium are
with Enalpril Maleate
mere hexasyllabic terms—
boring and too quantitative
to inspire the racing heart's
atrial fibrillation.
There is something to seven
that is not Greek or Latin,
English or Icelandic Verse.
So I'll take my medicine
as molecular metrics
to entrain my tossing heart.

MYSTICISM AND SCIENCE

Yes, I see angels, even Djinn,
and one Spiritual Guide who told me
when I asked him his name that I
could never pronounce its many
syllables in nano-microtime,
that like a Dolphin's sequenced clicks,
I would not be able to hear
the beats in time, the shifts in tone.
I thought of long Sri Lankan names
that sound like a tabla playing
in uneven rhythmic fractions
my hands could never duplicate.
And, yes, I know what brain science
would say about lucid dreaming—
I've even met the scientists,
and I'm OK with all of †hat.
Even if I can't ballroom dance,
play a two-handed instrument,
or speak two languages at once,
I can think two philosophies
happily at once—a threesome
of two beautiful women—
muses of yoga and science
in some Khajuraho embrace.
So, yes, I start by observing
my breath, my thoughts, and then my dreams
in the first hypnagogic state,
which, frankly, is more intensely

vivid than many academic
committee meetings I have had
to sit in with the likes of you.
The likes of angel, Djinn, and Guide
transcend the art of theatre
and show me things I do not know:
other worlds, music of the spheres,
or intercourse with *Apsaras*—
she alone was worth the hours
when nothing was going on in
your usual Zen Buddhist way
of dismissing all the above
as *makyo* and delusions.
I've never taken LSD
or psychedelic mushrooms,
but I know what deliriums
are like, so I know, that all this
could just be the brain's chemistry,
but, have you ever stopped thinking
to see that you are only there
part of the time, but for the rest,
the brain is doing something else,
and that something is listening
to the mind of the universe
and translating subtle signals
into angels, Djinn, and ETs?
I get tired of just being me,
so watching this sure beats TV.

THE DRAGONFLY
AND THE HUMMINGBIRD

Both are swift, both are beautiful.
One eats blood-piercing mosquitoes
hiding in blades of foreign grass
wrongly planted in my backyard
of high Sierra desert rock,
pinyons, bee flowers, and cactus
with sparse strands of buffalograss.
The other eats only nectar
from our apple trees and garden.
What do the Djinn and Angels eat?

BACK STORY

Lucifer first indicted God
for the crime of Creation;
that is what the War in Heaven
was really all about, not Christ
and Lucifer's envy of him
as Dissenting Milton would have
us believe in *Paradise Lost*.
Lucifer claimed that Creation
was an ego trip completely
without compassion for others,
for their infinite suffering
as time-tortured lives worked toward
some slow and ponderous final good.
(You can see why Lucifer still
is the patron saint of lawyers.)
The angels having just endured
a series of universes
from Big Bang to Lights Out! were tired
of singing Hosannas of praise,
and leaned forward, listening hard
to the argument that Nothing
was the natural state of things.
Why should there be something instead
of the pure equilibrium
of an absolute timeless void?
The first universe ran on rails,
so completely predictable,

that even God got bored before
it went blandly dark entropic.
Now He had an idea of
an opposition of free will
and physical laws struggling
in love and hate to an unknown
end that not even God could know.
The angels could take on bodies
of galaxies, angels of dark
could become black holes with the goal
to see whether the stark outrage
of existing things could win out
over a perfect timeless peace.
The majority of angels
were with God for raw existence,
but in losing Lucifer vowed
to show them what suffering was
really like in crashed galaxies
and carefully tortured children.
It is now half-time in the game.
With home-advantage, the demons
are winning and weak humans are
called in to substitute for beasts.

HERRN WALTER BENJAMIN:
MOSCA, COLORADO

Scoured by sand the dead steel hulk
of the scrapped Ford pickup truck sits
awaiting its resurrection
as junk art; one door hangs broken
like an old swing the kids played on,
when they weren't throwing rocks, knocking
out the windows; sand now covers
the seats and the weeds are coming
up through the rusted-out floor boards
where the dried tumbleweed is stuck.
The closed two pump gas station in
this dust-deviled adobe town
is an open-air sculpture park.
Here abandoned machines can gain
an aura in the age of art.

A DIALOGUE OF SELF AND DAIMON

Self:

Now that the angel has shifted from me to you,
what use is there for me in your *alaya* store?
Why did you advance my time and take death over?
Why should you wait until I'm some senile duffer,
or is there something you still can be hoping for?

Daimon:

Even if you were to get your ego out of my way—
and you've only begun to get the feel of that,
your end is the most important part of the play,
for how you die marks the trail like the cougar's scat.

Self:

For a Daimon, that's really some earthy image.
Next you will be talking of football and scrimmage?

Daimon:

I owe it all to you and our hikes in Crestone,
when I kept that cat out of your Tenderfoot zone.

Self:

Not to mention the bears with their berry-filled piles,
the slinking coyotes with their Mona Lisa smiles.

Daimon:

If it is angels not animals on your mind,
then let's cut to the chase and the real reason—

if she is now linked to me—you feel left behind,
and death still gives you that elemental frisson.

Self:
When I die, she shifts automatically to you,
so since she's left, doesn't it mean we both are through?

Daimon:
How you die is important to the three of us.
You're right to see us together, waiting for you,
and to empty yourself and make space luminous
is precisely the thing that you now need to do.

Self:
Does entering death in managed IV dying
darken the stream we're to follow into the sun?

Daimon:
And puts thought in the way of translucent flying,
which is something, remember, you've already done.

Self:
Which is my point, since that's done, why am I still here?

Daimon:
To work through the body's hold in death you still fear.
When your mind is the mud, the stem, and the lotus
you will be free to die and not even notice.

THE JESTER'S MARGINALIA:
Three Translations from Old Irish,
Old English, and Old Norse

In the library of St. Gall there is an oddity in the Priscian Manuscript—already famous for its seventeen marginalia invocations of St. Bridget. Since the marginalium is written with the same hand in Old Irish, Old Norse, and Old English, it has always been assumed to be a forgery and some sort of Ossianic prank of a learned monk and fiendish librarian from a much later period. Consequently, the poems have never been published. It is possible that a monk of an earlier period might know Irish and Norse, but it is hard to believe he would also know the West Saxon dialect of Old English. And yet the peregrinatio was sacred to Irish monks, and so I like to imagine an Irish monk making his way from Clonmacnoise to Ripon after the Viking destruction of Lindisfarne and on to St. Gall, far from the sea. Each of the poems shows an independent Irish spirit, "thinking otherwise"—as Bishop Berkeley was to term it centuries later when he said: "We Irish think otherwise." It is clear in the second poem that the author was familiar with some version of Beowulf, oral or written, as the poem would appear to be spoken by Grendel, cursing his attacker before he dies. When I was living in Switzerland, a kind librarian, knowing that I was a poet, gave me a translation of the Jester's Marginalia—as he liked to call it—into German, and then I reworked his scholarly German into English.

1.

The moon is full, the wind down.
I fear the unheard frog drop
of oars on the still waters
of the wide sea-laned Shannon.
More than the bell of Matins,
I hark to the round tower.

2.

I am not   child of Cain!
Your Church   lies on stones
it cannot hear — cry nor scream.

Before you were,   Enoch's kin,
taken to heaven,   were made
great giants   from weak men.

No demon,   I am
first-born,   heaven bent.
You the mold   scraped off trees,

hairless pigs,   ape-men,
clouded seed,   cattle cunt,
foul creatures   of time and muck!

3.

Old am I now,
fared wide on seas
castled with ice,
frost on my beard
already white
in the white spray.
My name I lost
when the Æsir
flung me out
the tossing boat,
off Iceland's red
burning rivers,
took out my breath
under waters
cold and steaming
and put in me
their forms and words
unknown to man.
Under the waves,
I talked with seals,
lifting me up
to breathe the air.
Flat on black sand,
then could I hear
the mountains talk,

hammers of dwarves,
and high pitched Elves
with their gold harps
and their strung bows
moving in air,
riding the clouds.
I sailed again
as mountains burst,
loud in black smoke.
Nowhere the sun,
nowhere the stars.
Endless the seas,
endless the ice.

IONA

This Iona stone
I hold in my hand—
Precambrian Lewisian Gneiss—
has the characteristic banding
of black, green, white, and a slight flush of red.
It is among the oldest rocks on earth,
2700 million years old.
Perfectly oval and smoothly polished
by the waves of St. Martin's Cave
that faces the open Atlantic,
the stone appeared to me at low tide
alone among thousands
in a cave that must utter in the dark
a fricative chatter before
the stones are flooded by the sea
to rock back and forth
between the open vowels of the wind
and the closed consonant stone
in a tidal meditation of the ages—
of the sea, the magma,
the up-swelling crust
and the compressions
of metamorphic rock.
The elemental beings
who came here before us
are strongly present in these rocks.
With their solidly inhabited bodies,

they have no need of souls
transcendent and split off,
for they still ring with the echo
of the death of the star
that hurled them here
and are infinitely at one
with place as we are not.
Djinn or *Kami,* dwarfs or gnomes,
call them what you will,
but mind is in these rocks,
as much as in dragon-loved,
bright gem polished stones,
tourist Grand Canyons,
or this Hebridean spouting cave.

A PAGAN UR-TEXT OF
THE LEBOR GEBÁLA ÉRENN

Book One. The First World

In darkness I write, not the dark
of the flamed volcanic gods
who take summers' crops from men,
but of Brigid's templed womb.

Windowless, my earth-burmed hut;
empty of comforts, I wait
for the forehead eye to light
the way to Brigid's knowledge.

Nothing I touch can I take
—not pen, sword, or Druid staff.
only alone in the dark
can I sleepless dream and see.

Before time, before this sun
moved, before red Earth cooled,
we lived on a perfect star
in the perfect Pleiades.

We were gods and lived as gods,
knowing neither death nor pain,
but we lost knowledge of love,
of loss, sorrow, and remorse.

Our star died for us to send
us out in swirling metals
to an unborn denser sun
of chaos and storms of rock.

War was there then in heaven,
great collidings of the gods,
still children in their new minds
howling only for themselves.

Then came worlds where rocks had been.
Elementals were born in
earth, air, fire, and water--
these the spirits before Man.

Then came the life of the sea,
animal, plant, clear blue sky,
and light in which all were seen
in seeded copulations.

The bodiless clouds above
looked on coupling animals
and knew desire and lusted
to have springtime sex in them.

In showers of gold they rained
into lizard seed and egg.
At pleasure's end, they could not
ascend to be gods again.

Sad beasts screamed, trapped gods cried out.
Minotaur and centaur,
chimeras roamed earth and sea..
From this race Man was to come.

Book Two. The Second World

The gods found no peace in beasts.
Some forgot, becoming beasts,
more cruel and resentful,
no longer knowing themselves.

Others discovered the dream
that set them free nights to be
up in the skies, free again
to command beasts of the day.

Then the meteor struck earth
and the gods discovered death
bore all the freedom of dreams
and built their kingdom of death.

To live was to be asleep.
To be dead and dream-bodied
was the real life the gods
enjoyed while the beasts endured.

When warm blooded animals
gave off the odor of sex,
the gods were startled again
and hovered, sniffing over them.

Again the gods took over
the hot animal bodies
and coupled with them for play.
Thus the walking apes were born

The apes dreamed the dreams of gods,
the gods dreamed of being apes,
so in Ethiopia,
the race of Man first was born.

Then continents ripped apart,
seas shifted and Man began
his hard life of wandering,
day-dreaming and night thinking.

Book Three. The Third World

The long Age of Ice began.
Man wandered, following herds
of reindeer, bison, auroch,
and the great-tusked mastodon.

Man drove out the Great Cave Bear
from his lair, took on his fur,
and placed his skull on altars
of square, unhewn flat stone.

Man found in the warm traces
of the animals red capped
mushrooms men chewed together
as their souls were born in caves.

The animals were Man's life--
gods and Man as one again.
Aloneness opened, shamans,
men in animal skins, painted

the dreaming on the rock walls,
carved animals of amber,
engraved Goddess images
that girls signed with menstrual hands.

The squat men who could not run,
but tottered from side to side,

could not follow us dream-bodied
to animal gatherings.

We left them behind, dull louts
of crude tools and ugly hags—
sullen, without Brigid's star
of knowledge on their foreheads.

They backed off in fear from us,
hunted rabbits, disappeared
into the southern passes,
and left no carved marks behind.

Then the skies changed, ice melted,
and the seas rose covering
our seasonal fishing camps.
This world ended in Flood.

Book Four. The Fourth World

From islands at the world's edge,
the College of Wizards stood.
When the World Flood recalled it,
they were released from hiding

and again allowed to take
a hand in the affairs of men.

Before, no temples were built.
Now temples began to rise.

From green Ethiopia
they had come an age ago.
Now to Anatolia
they called for a Gathering

of all the tribes and schools
of star diviners, wizards
who became lion or eagle
to run and dream-fly at night.

Wizard now challenged shaman,
on hilltops built Goddess Wombs
with great stone plinths, each engraved
with animals of each tribe:

fox, leopard, lizard, ostrich,
headless dancers of the dead.
The stars took their positions,
rising on the horizons.

The shamans lost the contest,
and left for the Northern Lights
where there were no sunken caves,
but oceans of endless ice.

There at the Crossroads arose
the school of the new Druids,
the parting of all the tribes,
each with its god to guide them.

Then the Druids named a king,
and feast of the sacred bull.
All drank the blood, ate the meat,
and swore faith to the year's king.

When the *Temuir* Feis ended,
the Chosen became blessed to Death,
the king rose from the dead bull
and coupled with the Goddess.

In the morning the tribes left.
Indra led the way eastward
for the horses and cattle,
his mind set on the mountains.

Dagda led the slow way back,
westward across the broad lands
turning from open tundra
to the short sight lines of trees.

Lir led the way to the sea,

on rock island stepping stones
from Aegean to Malta,
and starred Hyperborea.

Long before the tribes had come
to Eriu they had known
one another from the depths
of time before history.

I fostered child of Brigid,
raised among the Western Norse,
son of a priestess mother,
raped and taken from Temuir,

here alone on this west shore
declare the Lebor to be
a monkish fraud only meant
to advance the evil Church.

May earthquakes strike their churches,
may winds erase their black words,
may rising seas again flood
their towered monuments.

I see in Brigid's forehead eye
the coming age ending not

merely by skyrock and flood
but by volcanoes, earthquakes,

storms and seas rising against
all the cities of the world.
A thousand years from today
this cursed monkish age will end.

I the unnamed of the *filidh*,
of no man's world recite this,
knowing I will never see
in light what I see in dark.

SLIPPING ON ICE

Have you noticed pain's
a way of paying
attention to life's
elemental acts:
bending to pick up
something on the floor,
getting up from bed,
or grunting, annoyed
at the traffic stop
of an obdurate stool?
Just an unseen glaze
of ice on four steps,
you slip up in air,
hitting the top stair
with the thick muscle
of your left Lat, glad
it was not your neck.
Now pain brings you back
to paying attention
to each move of life.
At lunch the bright blue
of her lively eyes
also slips you up,
and you hit the facts
of life hard—time scarred.
You're old and she's young.
It hurts because you

were not watching out
for the shadowed ice
you were standing on,
caught up as you were
over wine at lunch
by the high fullness
of her sweatered breasts.
Let them be. You're not
in time for them now.
Pay strict attention
to this thick instant:
an old man who feels
as she leans her breast
under her red coat
against your coat's sleeve,
distracted from pain,
watching how she looks
at antique silver
on a winter's walk
in the restored old
town of Lambertville.

THE PINK CONCH

At ease in the early
Hawaiian afternoon,
aloft in a Manoan
tree house on a green hill
overlooking Waikiki,
I linger between her knees
and gaze at the pink conch
and listen to the leaves.
Nature must love this form,
granting it to orchid,
sea shell and this open
entrance of florid life.
Painterly the colors
vary from red to pink
and shades of pinkish beige.
Red frightens me—a slash
of the wound that heals
in lunar mysteries;
beige is Earth's sandalwood,
but pink recalls the sea.
And then there is the scent!
from French egg mayonnaise
to fish or funky cheese,
depending on the hold
of inner candida
and bacterial trace.
But one there was who kept

a musky pheromone
turbulence triggering
wild primordial scent.
This is the one woman
I can never forget.
An aeon from this time,
exiled to a dark burnt-out
rotating neutron star
for inappropriate
thoughts like these I will not
be thinking of Earth's trees,
but meditating on
the musky odor of her
wild transcendental cunt.

MEDITATION ON A ROMAN MURAL FROM POMPEY

Quim is a loving word,
vibrating on the lips—
an AUM of adoration.
Cunt is a curse word
spoken more with teeth than lips—
an explosive breath,
the grunting sneer
of primitive horseback riders
who took their females
crudely from the back
and kept their distance.
They did not look
their women in the eyes.
In hot Africa where the females
had steatopygous buttocks,
the male rod had to be long
to get by all that fat
and reach deep inside,
but for Ice Age creatures
who wrapped arms and legs
around one another to keep warm
there were no buttocks to get by,
and such long rods would tear
the cervix and rip up the womb.
Sex switched from stallions
with long rods mounting mares
and violent teeth biting necks

in violent possession
to lingering penetration.
The entrance became its own place
and just not a passage way.
Pussy is a visual word—
a furry little creature
to treasure and caress,
a fossil-word that records the shift
to frontal embrace.
Vulva is spoken with the tongue
and the breath going in and out—
an aveolar touch, lingering
to allow the breath in
along with the scent of her
through the nostrils—
the gnosis of who she really is—
the prelude to the flutter of the tongue
over the clitoris of an artist
who begins to play her
as the musical instrument
God intended her to be
by putting more nerves there
than in any other part
of the human body.
God damn all the cultures that dare
cut this Eye of God out.

SUNT LACIMAE RERUM
ET MENTEM MORTALIA TANGUNT.

One sign of isolate old age
is to turn over memories
like clippings pasted to a page—
still shots taken from old movies.

I don't know if I am sorry,
recalling adulterous acts,
lost in *monono aware*,
or just collecting artifacts.

You lift your feet, knees together,
to put your pink underpants on,
and your thighs compress your lower
lips to form a pearl helicon

that cannot liquidate your fear
of being overwhelmed again;
I see this white pearl as my tear
that we'll never make love again.

JOINED BODIES, SEPARATED MINDS, SUMMER 1976

It is a warm summer night
and the humid air flashes
with a few slow fireflies.
We have left our beach cabins
to make love in the moonless
night air, hidden from the sight
of the other summer guests.
At the edge of the field
we smell the honeysuckle
and lie down close to its vines.
She comes at once, eyes astonished,
as I extend into her.
Looking at her exalted
face under me as her eyes
widen in awe, I listen
as she becomes taken up
by the stars that I can see
reflected in her dark eyes.
My back is turned from heaven,
but her body's full embrace
is heaven enough for me.
Seeing the stars within her,
smelling the honeysuckle,
and feeling my own honey
flowing into her flower,
I delight in her as she

gasps again in an orgasm
caused by mine inside hers.
She and I and the field
lose our embodied edges.
Audible flowers, firefly
stars, honeysuckled stamen,
bodies absolved of limits
become one topology--
an interpenetrating
paradise for Solomon
and Sheba and a palace
for redeemed Adam and Eve.
All this, she explains to me
almost forty years later
is not at all how she would
describe what went on in her.

DAS EWIG-WEIBLICHE ZIEHT UNS HINAN

For God's sake, man, don't write love poetry!
No one writes that sort of thing anymore.
The Eternal Feminine is dated
like wigs, *Sturm und Drang*, and Goethe.
All that New Age slop is a compost heap
of myths and outdated Romantic kitsch
about Brigid, Gaia, and Sophia.
Feminists and PoMo critics will have
your crotch apophysis on a platter.
You should know by now the Feminine is
just camouflage for male domination.
Write a love poem now, and your lover
will be the first to kick you out of bed
and let you know that is not how she felt
on your poetically transfigured night.

Men and women live in separate worlds
and imagination keeps them apart.
It's like watching my neighbor's huge TV
through my kitchen window across our street.
She sees a single connected story,
but I see only a kaleidoscope
of rapidly changing colored patterns.
She is in her world, and I am in mine.
Were we lovers the story in her mind
and the images in mine would not have

the same plot-line and the same conclusion.
Surfaces keep pulling us together,
but for all of our wet adhesive sex,
we cannot agree on what it really meant—
a stream, or a marriage of dried cement.

THE FACTS OF LIFE

Living things grow
from slow to fast

until what's now
becomes what's past.

When there' so many,
none can value any.

You might say
it's just God's way,

but I wouldn't
and you shouldn't.

Fire consumes flame,
no one's to blame.

No rock was hurled
at our world,

the reason why
things now die

comes when millions,
become billions.

The air gets hot,
oceans rot

with only shit
to inhabit

folks start to cough
and then die off.

MEDICAL RECORDS

The difficulties of illness:
at eleven, the black panic
under ether, the dark crushing
spiral turning me inside out.

At eighteen the pain of waking—
after twelve hours of surgery—
without drugs, the surgeon's anger
at the nurses, demanding they
inject me immediately,
and I, delighting in codeine's
sweat, aloft in opiate trance,
explored the pleasures of the mind.

After cancer came open heart
surgery and a bovine valve—
all the tubes in my chest--weak in
the old effort for existence;
no injected trance opiates
this time, just cold, safe pain-killers.

Kidney collapse and tetany
proved to be as hard to endure:
the Santa Fe doctors could not treat
two afflictions at once and so
discharged me from the hospital
without water in high noon's heat
where I collapsed and was brought back,

babbling in broken syllables—
glossalalia of hollow ghost—
while a dull misery flooded
all the muscles of my body.
But was it my body when I
had two minds in delirium?
I could dream while awake and be
In India and Santa Fe,
talking to nurses and hearing
a flute play in Varanasi
for a Ganges robed funeral
that could have been my own since I
saw all of it at once above
as the high calcium flooded
the synapses and doubled me,
eliminating the neural wall
that insulated one from two.
Do we fall in love, mistaking
in Plato's myth of Orphic egg,
the lover for our lost double?
Whenever I come close to death,
I am not what I think I am.

THE DEATH OF NEDA

The whites of her eyes rolled up like a saint
in a filmed drama of staged yogic bliss,
then her head turned and showed it was not paint
that guttered out. The sniper did not miss,
in spite of Neda's black Persian Hijab,
the perfect placing of his pervert's kiss,
but he was just doing his Basij job;
the street was not the place for their complaint.
Religion is the robed disguise of thugs,
whether snipers on the roofs shooting girls,
Taliban buying guns by selling drugs,
West Bank settlers with their Uzis and curls
    stealing wells with walls and Adonai's will,
    who gave them the land and license to kill.

PLAYING AROUND WITH SONNETS

Variation on Sonnet 163 by Francisco de Aldana

What causal chain, Daimon, is iron set
that lovers caught nude in Hephaistos' net
struggle with tongues, arms and long legs enchained
in a jasmine nest by sharp thorns constrained?
And what vital breath through lips that both take,
crying and gasping as they dream awake,
in the blossomed night's dark odored pleasure
the rude husband's dawn in equal measure.

Love, my lovely Phyllis, in this strong hold
is forging my silver with your bright gold,
and the iron chain your husband has wrought
is a blacksmith's work dishonestly bought.
    Fathers contract marriages for their own gains,
    Lovers forge golden bonds from their cold chains.

QUESTION TO EXTREMEOPHILES

Does beauty lurk in black sea thermal vents?
Do those tubes with their waving tendrils thrill
transfigured by sulfidic sacraments
in some interior hooded clitoral
molecular chemistry of ion
gates of sound rather than perceptual space?
A whole world exists down there—like Titan
or Enceladus—where darkness is chaste.
What we have known as the world is not
even true for ours much less Saturn's moons.
From arctic ice, desert sands, Yellowstone's hot
springs to cosmic rayed stratosphere balloons,
    life is an inevitable fumble,
      whenever molecules wildly tumble.

THE HAND

The hand with its tight opposable thumb
has a curiously prehensile task,
whose reach for apple or atomic bomb
exceeds its thick comprehensible grasp.
It was once a fin without a firm link,
sea-formed in the dark company of swarms
in depths to which it could easily sink.
Perhaps that is why we name weapons arms.
Between the two limbs, the pendulous dick
is straightforward and never seeks to hold;
it knows its place is peripatetic—
a horned ram to be released in the fold.
   Our members seem always partial to wholes
   inserted or enveloping other souls.

BOLIDES AND VOLCANOES

Dr. Tollmann stumbled upon a bolide
that knocked the oceans up to old Salt Lake,
before Indians and Mormons chose to make
their homes close to where volcanoes reside.
Since Lyell and Darwin we all believe
in a slow and steady growth called progress,
but Earth was never granted a reprieve
from the Asteroids' erratic egress.
When a bolide hit and sent refugee
mobs from Palestine to Ain Ghazal,
the Aegean poured into the Black Sea
and a tsunami's seizure of Grand Mal
    wiped out Knossos, and let Moses escape.
    Mars lost life. Something out there now takes shape.

THE NEW AGE CULT OF 2012

There are cycles within cycles, the Maya say,
some are within the sun, others the Milky Way.
Five thousand one hundred and twenty four years prod
this inner cycle of the sun; only a god
knows the long count of the faults of our galaxy
where strange attractors of occult dark gravity
tear open our tectonic plates and breaking crust
to hot zones of magma and volcanic upthrust.
Legends of lost continents appeal to crazies,
casting oracles like tearing petals from daisies
to know if their god forgives and will rapture them,
or if they should freeze themselves in Raëlian phlegm,
    and thus be given an apocalyptic pass
     and be granted eternity for their sad ass.

NATURE

Scientists say that love is merely chemistry,
With serotonin up here, pheromones down there.
Astrophysics says all is space and gravity,
Not Jehovah's *fiat* or *dicta obiter*.
I have read in *Nature* that galaxies collide,
That Andromeda is heading for our Milky Way.
One wonders what happens for life forms caught inside
Planets knocked up in F. Crick's panspermia way.
I feel like a bad dream frightened child at midnight
Who comes upon his nude parents struggling in bed
And doesn't know what to make of the troubling sight
Of Daddy hurting Mommy, her eyes closed in dread.
    Perhaps if galaxies collide in slow stellar time,
    Their long ecstatic fuck partakes of the sublime.

THE ANT

Maybe when we look at an ant we're not
seeing an individual being—
a communist contentedly living
for needs, not hoping for more than he's got.
Maybe it's merely one single neuron
in the nest's highly distributed brain.
Did the learned scientists on Krypton
choose Earth because ants had learned to entrain
the Many in One long before Plato?
The Buddha tried to teach proud, grasping men,
taking Sankhya and turning it to Zen,
that Self was not worth the bother to know.
   If by boiling water it turns to air,
     maybe hot selves are neurons unaware.

A DANDELION

If a self is formed to favor itself
more effectively than a feint in light
of tender obliging considerate leaves
who'd thrust no place on continental shelf,
nor claim on distant islands their birth right
with seeds clinging to shores in tidal heaves;
if nature born in bacterial spawn
in thermal vents, desert sand, and arctic ice
shows no regard for self-less courtesy—
to play croquet on smoothly leveled lawn,
or gamble without chance with weighted dice,
or cover fists with gloved diplomacy,

    this dandelion breaking through concrete
    is life's answer to Buddha's middle street.

CHOIR BOYS

Not the organ answering Job out of the whirlwind,
nor the tiny pointed notes of the harpsichord—
metallic and discrete as knights in armories
unfurled and elevated above the clubbed blood
of churlish battle or bones struck on mammoth skulls,
nor the sun's arteries drained in stained glass truncheons;
bound in cassocks to their claustral occulted place
where priestly functions anoint the choir boys' throats
in Borborite eucharist older than the Mass
cherub buttocks lean on the misericord's hard love
tangled in wings of the dove and coils of the snake
that soon break sunset's shaft on the rising full moon;
    but now the pianoforte in thundering halls
    breaks the hold in revolution's noisy applause.

SURFING THE WEB

Artillery shells on the Buddha's Bamyan cliff,
Talibanic acid flung in the veiled schoolgirl's face,
Qaeda beheadings taped for a medieval riff
streamed with the web's "*Allahu Akbar's*" podcast trace.
Words alone among the silences they lattice
in sleepless nights in the world wide web's tendrils
conjure Fatehpur Sikri's red sandstone palace
where Islam arched religions with Sufi spandrils.
Akbar's grieving shade waits in the Diwan, alone.
In Waziristan, CIA drones fly above
in the full moonlight on the huts of sand and stone,
circling coils of the serpent on wings of the dove.
　　　Towers fall; ruins stand. Our oil-derricked lyres
　　　Untune the sky as Gaza burns in brimstone fires.

CATEGORY MISTAKES ARE POETRY IN THE MAKING

This poem is not about a poem
about a pipe that is a brown painted
canvas to bring its layered message home,
rather it is a gesture lightly feignted--
one not really Dada or surreal--
but something closer to code turned symbol
that suddenly like a koan makes you feel
the images of needle and thimble
are medieval Alibgensian echoes
of phallus and vulva, dagger and cup,
grail and bleeding spear and, God only knows,
pukku and *mikku,* stick and Stanley Cup!
    No, this poem is a condensation—
    category's transubstantiation.

MONONO AWARE

I had heard about Earth,
but did not believe it—
all those mumblings about
evil as the primal
plot of every art—
torture twisted governments.
The stories seemed too bad
to be true, so I found
myself a way to slip
on a human body
in the odd moves of sex
and went slumming into
matter's duality.
It was just as they said,
only worse than I'd thought.
I can't wait to get out.
Yet there were those moments—
so different from light
oscillating only
in cool celestial white,
the blue New England sky
in slanted autumn light,
the colored abundance,
or naked Britt running
into the pool alone
under the waterfall
on green Molokai'i—
all calendar clichés
that were right about time.

A MATTER OF SCALE

Galaxies too are hurricanes—
black holes their quiet lightless eyes.
We live as life spun on debris.
African bacteria thrive
in the water drops that fall on
Texas and Louisiana.
The red spot of Jupiter is
a centuries enduring storm.
And we think Man is the measure
of all things! We're the measurer
of everything—little schoolboys
who use their rulers to measure
in inches their erected dicks.

THE END

So is it Big Crunch
or simply Lights Out!
The scientists demur.
Whatever way you
like to look at it,
what you can't see counts—
dark matter, that is.
Personally, I'm
all right with Lights Out!
from on high or with
kinks underneath space.
Think of light as God's
bright ejaculate—
quantum foam as cum,
particles as sperm
inside female space,
dark only from our
thick male point of view.
Prudes have got it wrong,
ancients had it right,
sex itself is our
earthy sacrament.
The dark matter takes
the imprint of light
when some adjacent
fractal bubble of
another universe

bumps up against ours.
Then the dark contracts
into a single
singularity.It only needs God's
thought to prick the light
on thickened nothing
to spark a Big Bang
all over again.
O strung melodies,
what the right hand plays,
the left hand endows.

EMILY AT AMHERST

Whenever Emily attracted in
To her singled crowded room
Errant angel and storied jinn,
Antic poetry began to loom:

Not the cart's trochaic chant
Nor the cantered anapestic trot,
And not the preacher's pious rant—
Sounding brass for what men begot.

She was a prophetess of trains,
Whose sudden starts and instant stops
Her vatic maddened dash contains—
Flowering weeds in fields of crops.

Emily tied infinity in knots
And her tight poetry in packets—
A bumble bee that nectar besots,
or conferenced crows enjoying rackets.

Emily was all imp and devil,
Grace's angel and Earth's elemental.
Amherst's hermit could pray in revel—
Our most playful Transcendental.

---

[1] See Hilary Thompson, "The Mad Dash," Undergraduate Paper submitted to the Department of English, University of Toronto, 1986.

QUANTUM ENTANGLEMENT

Next life I want to be smarter.
I'm reading Nature on quantum
entanglement and listening
to Monk and Coltrane together
entangling at Carnegie Hall
with two themes at once: "Tea for Two"
and "Sweet and Lovely." So who's first?
Einstein, Podolsky, and Rosen
in *Nature* in 1935,
or Whitehead's refutation
of ideas of "simple location"
in *Science and the Modern World*
at Harvard in 1929?
or should I go back before Jazz
to the music of Charles Ives'
several bands playing at once,
or Erik Satie's typewriters
clanking noisily in *Parade*,
or the multiple perspectives
of Wölfli, Braque, and Picasso?
You see my problem? I don't read
music or math, so I don't know
what the fuck I'm talking about,
yet I can hear, see, and think it,
but that just makes me feel stupid.
I wish the scholars would write real
history and show how Bebop

and the Birth of the Cool relate
Shannon's information theory
and New York's Macy Conferences
to Monk's flat-fingered chopped chords
and Coltrane's micro sequences.
Ideas seem to get around
space under time in latticed spin.

LA ESCRITURA DEL DIOS

I once heard Borges at Harvard—
he who prophesied the terror
of fractals before Mandelbrot
wrote out his Zahir equation,
tapped Enter with his computer
and saw imprisoned infinity
rattle its chains—Rilke's panther
and blind Borges'scripted tiger
paced endlessly, writing the lines
unread on their staring eyes.

BEDTIME STORY FOR ANDROIDS

Unintentional as black asteroids
knocked about in the cluttered Kuiper Belt,
organic molecules hitchhike on rocks—
themselves the debris of shattered planets—
that pebble skip on gravity's fields
until their lurching drunk's stumbling random walk
becomes defined as meteor showers
settling down on the floors of acrid seas
of hot outgassing volcanic planets
that take them turning dead junk into life.

TO THE ISRAELIS AND PALESTINIANS

My freckled soul has felt
its share of Eastern light,
but none of your praying
seems to stir God to come
into Jihad's whirlwind
or West Bank settlements,
nor can Christian churches,
paved with rapt donations
make God's Light compliant
to stained glass and sandstone.
To clear a future free
of religions' scripted hate
we need to open up
the world to those who
really need it and not
make war on those who hold
the past because they can't
endure the present day.

DIGITAL GOVERNMENT:
HOMAGE TO GEORGE ORWELL,
PHILIP K. DICK, AND WENDELL BERRY

It's less an Act
than some survey,
a faceless *Facebook* fact

from those who prey
through an algorithm
that can precisely say

what's in your jism,
how your genes denote
though Google's prism

the guns you tote,
your chosen porn
from anal to Deep Throat.

Once you're born,
digits do the work
while you're on the horn.

With smart phones
the NSA and CIA
run by Skull and Bones

get you to pay
for tracking devices
that let you play

games with your vices,
but if numbers iterate,
profiling some crisis,

your own smart phone
tells the Directorate
to send a bee-sized drone.

URSCHREI

Was it the fear of changed faces
that taught the first art of reading,
before there were tracks on the ground
or prophetic tooth-marks on bone?
The word hit onto hard named things,
starting to beat sense into sound,
one thing coupled to another.
Repetition but not yet rhyme
evolved at first, pleased with itself,
as the word would come back and back—
stick on hollow resounding wood,
or bone on sun-bleached mammoth skull.
At first, poems celebrated
the killing of beasts struck with words,
only much later the sunrise
or the full moon's nocturnal light.
Can there again be poetry
without personality's moods—
Cézanne's apples' pure Being—
ripe things possessed by raw color?

CÉZANNE

Objects
intimately inclined
to the spaces
of one another.

Planes aslant,
geometry breaking up
in grief for ripening things.

Only apples on a table.

Color is its own
seizure of possession,
not a predicate
of fruit, plate, or table.

A rainbow is
and is not—
a matter of angles,
of sun and observer,
and water-bearing clouds.

These apples are
whatever Being is.

AN APOLOGY TO KENNETH REXROTH

diversae varie viae reportant

It is, as it should be, old soul,
that you do not remember me.
We were only for the moment
passengers crossing traveled lives,
intent on separate arrivals.
You came to read your poems aloud
amid the technic distractions
of MIT where I had come
to teach cultural history.
Not senior in rank, I was asked
to drive you in November's rain
through dimly lit suburban streets
for a night at Wellesley College.
Enclosed in the academic car
of my small VW Square Back,
I did most of all the talking
as you endured yet another
young poet trying to put forth
his case when it was not yet time.
You were polite, not listening
to the words, but the cadence,
and the windshield's slapped metronome.
Then you cut in, interrupting:
"You know you have a wonderful
spoken Anglo-Irish diction."

I was startled. The dead were pleased.
My Irish grandmother was glad
that the child she had not known
had felt her longing to return.

What could I say to Rexroth's shift
to the dark matter underneath
the burnt architecture of stars?
Invocations of fawning praise,
or recitals of influence?—
of how in my sophomore year,
with *The Phoenix and the Tortoise*
and *Romancero Gitano*,
I had been caught by the Urtext
of the octosyllabic line—
the slow measured tread of the horse—
four hoof beats, pause, and four again—
Verde viento. Verdes ramas.—
the tread of the Troubadours, ude
strung across their backs, returning
from the Crusades with Persian verse,
Arabic songs and drummed *stampies*.
Of course, I was to mind all that
later, but it came to me then—
voweled with Rexroth and Lorca.
Now that you are dead and I am
at sixty-eight left to myself,

I think of you and your reserve.
Please forgive me for sending you
my poems, for not understanding
the meaning of that enclosure—
intimate and anonymous—
in which we passed alone in life.
Young poets, never send your poems
to older and well-known poets.
Forsake ambition and the lust
for attention from multitudes.
Wait, as my grandmother waited,
through lives and deaths, above it all,
in expectation not of fame,
but the isolated moment
when two souls pass apart in dark,
nodding as they part their own time.

REMEMBERING A NIGHT
WITH STOCKHAUSEN

Music draws the soul; unearthly music
tears the soul from the flayed-open body—
as Marsyas learned from a mad goddess.
Wolves and lunatics howl at the full moon,
but those who hear the songs of their lost stars
die like lovers with broken open hearts.
Rilke called it *Sehnsucht*, I call it *Hörsucht*.
Stockhausen told me he awoke hearing
Egyptian star music from Sirius.
I am not that Pharoahonic, my home
is the Pleiades' unseen seventh star.
When the constellation awakens me
at its zenith on a clear winter's night,
I know what it means to be exiled, locked
into a dense body on a planet
where violence is thought entertaining.
Stockhausen said, before his *Jahreslauf*
was to be performed that night in Paris,
that our Earth was a penal colony
for criminal souls in our galaxy.
And so here I am, listening to Bach
and thinking he alone should be enough
to win humanity's pardoned release.

AFTER CLOSING BLUES

(In memory of Bill Evans, while listening to
Cyrus Chestnut's *The Dark before the Dawn*)

I don't know what to be—
F minor or the key of C.

Am I done or undone,
or earthworms in the sun?

I've been where others were,
got degrees and tenure.

Women knew parts of me,
most only partially.

Friends were never near,
more air as atmosphere.

If making love or war
just goes to change the score

in a game I'm not playing,
why then am I staying?

La commedia é finita,
e la via é smarrita.

Am I bleeding in the tub,
or alone in this empty club?

Who plays himself the blues
until the shift of crews?

The singer has gone to sleep
with the owner for her keep,

and there's nothing at home
in New York or Old Rome,

but an empire on the brink
and dirty dishes in the sink.

3:00 AM BLUES

Rain drops
gutters drip
sibilant tires hiss
or make a splash
hit or miss
in a puddle
splatter-dash
every movement
is getting
somewhere
being inclined
and intent
but my desires
get me nowhere
unaligned
and in a muddle
I write in lines
giving meaning
to small things
that could not
care less
for my designs
or their stress
in being more
than they are
they won't serve
as metaphor

tires or car
and are not
at home
in an Asian poem
or Shakti-begot
in Tantric dreaming
words can thrive
on their own
raindrops
are raindrops
and nothing more
I am alive
not for
Cornell's archive
each thought drips
filling nothing
without a sound
or any splashes
but my heart skips
in the morning
will I be found
fit for ashes
or the ground

A LAZY SUMMER AFTERNOON

spent listening to Chet Baker
crooning "You Don't Know What Love Is,"
and of course thinking of you
always with the large family
your generous life is built upon.
I am over your horizon,
in a side world with other stars
in unsettling constellations
that do not spell out home
but do convince me that I am
not who I think I am and you are
a part of what I can't recall.
We have written into our lives
sheet music for popular songs,
but the sad trumpet slides off key
and the piano player hears
notes from other songs and might riff
off into other melodies
did not the human voice keep him
within its love story of loss.
This is where you and I come in
from God knows where in our timed lives
that no longer keep to the line
they once did before we listened
to the star voices in our eyes.
There is nothing we can do now.
We are impossibilities

to one another, openings
to uninhabitable lives.
Baker's muted trumpet returns
to the well populated song,
the piano sadly gives in,
and I am left again alone,
recalling what we never were.

PANTOUM

Chill autumn's air is in this August night.
The evenings shorten in Maine's northern light.
I fear another winter like the last.
My life is writing memoirs of the past.

The evenings shorten in Maine's northern light.
Soon the inns will close, the song birds take flight.
Last winter you too flew to Baja's sea.
I learned then how much was taken from me.

I fear another winter like the last.
I am an old man by Eros miscast.
When you are gone I will be boarded up.
Blue seas will turn gray and dark clouds build up.

My life is writing memoirs of the past.
You are now storm weather in my forecast.
Your life fills up and takes you from my sight.
Chill autumn's air is in this August night.

THE DARK WINTER AFTERNOONS
IN PORTLAND

Dark energy around black hole
transports my dimensionless soul
into light wormholing its way
through what space-time I cannot say.

My I need not survive this shift,
and can be left behind to drift
as traces of gas and dark light
future stars can use to ignite.

But in this dark time remaining,
I will watch without complaining,
surfaces of sun and earth turn
their insides out with time to burn.

Civilizations come apart,
religion kills science and art,
and in the management of lies
politicians consume the skies.

The sun burns the cold mountain tops,
the arctic ice pulls out the stops,
the coastlines sink, the Great Plains flood,
the Gulf fills up with toxic mud.

In such a dark enlightening time,
blindness to Dharma is a crime.
The force of truth now transpires
in storms and floods and forest fires.

IT'S TIME

Yes, there's time,
but I'm not really into it.

The thing about me
is that things
are just stuff around me—
barnacles on a whale.

But I am stuck on something else.
and then I am completely out of it.
Now you know why
I keep talking
about tesseracts and hyperspheres,
and sex.

Sex grounds me
and gives me someone
I can really get into.

Trouble is sex usually
gets all fucked up in time.

I keep looking for
someone I can really make it with
in time and out,
but even Fra Angelico's angel
can't get his wings into the box
Mary is packaged in.

Projecting all this on you
is definitely not going to get me anywhere.
Try bottling the blue of the sky—
or your breath for that matter—
it's like settling down on the horizon—
move in and it moves out.

It completely screws up time with things
that have nothing to do with it.

So let's be love,
instead of me being
in love with you.

You've got a real garden
and don't need to crush
pretty flowers to dry in a poetry book.

RETIRED

Alone,

silence curled
cat-like
around time.

Nothing remains
to be done
about tomorrow.

The edges of me
fade off
into soft felt
invisibilities.

I begin to be
things stopped me
from being.

Now is no longer
just a clock tick
between
two black lines.

BEATRICE, SUMMER 1977

When it is evening and all the vowels are out
unconsonant in the open warm summer air,
I dream of writing poems in Italian where rhymes
fall easily off the vines laden with grape tropes
and *proseco* foams over uncorked passages,
and full breasts spill out over the small tops of light
summer dresses like the blue Guatemalan print
spaghetti-strapped dress Beatrice was wearing
as she bent over me and our abundance burst.
As humming birds are with flowers she was with me.
I shall always pronounce her name in Italian,
singing the four vowels in a *passacalgia*
through Tuscan narrow streets, celebrating her breasts
while the cupped vowels caressed by the consonants
remain within their evening stroller's glad love song
as the sun glides from blue skies to lined horizons.

FOR BEATRICE, OCTOBER, 2013

Autumn again—
beauty's attractor
into an age of ice.

Each autumn now
could be my last.
We met in a Scottish autumn
of yellow Larkspurs and gorse
and purple heather
thirty-seven years ago.
Now we complete our marriage
no longer bound
to raising a child,
running a household
or our Mom and Pop
summer camp of Lindisfarne
high in the Sangre de Cristo mountains.
In love's final ablation of the body
we wait for one
or the other of us to die first.

Nothing is left
to say about the leaves.
Portland's autumn foliage
does not turn colors all at once
in a Vermont calendar fall,
but individually,
tree by tree,
and so do we.

BOOK TWO

A PORTLAND CALENDAR

"WELCOME TO MAINE"

Everybody says it in quotes—
not in Boston, not Manhattan;
but then I've come here in May's spring
and know nothing of Maine's winter.
Azaleas and Forsythia,
pink Magnolias and Daffodils
are out at once with cherry trees.
Portland has now no rain or fog.
Maine is shorts and Tee shirt happy
enough to call this spring summer.
Santa Fe was medically denied
to me and Crestone kicked me out
with Zen altitude and collapse
in kidneys' failure and calcium's
wild delirium and mad trance.
This land of painters and poets--
free of the shadow of Harvard
and memories of M.I.T--
is a new life in a new land.
        Incipit vita nova.

ON MOVING INTO PORTLAND, MAINE AND READING TWO ANTHOLOGIES OF NEW ENGLAND POETRY

If we cut out nature,
tourist calendar art,
housewives staring out—
hands in the Puritan
stocks of the kitchen sink—
as their sullen husbands
put on their pick-up trucks
like overalls of rust,
fresh mud and old manure,
nothing much is left for
Creative Writing profs.
I turn to a new book
by China's Yang Lian,
a high diplomat's son,
born in Berne, who had lived
on the same street I did.
Lost in translation, I
wander around his poems.
They've gone off in English:
John Ashbery's abstract
painterly poetry
crossed with a Beat poet's
cascade of metaphors—
the declamatory
rhetoric of Ginsberg

and metal versed rock stars.
Stars are not rocks, they are
thermonuclear fires
set by demiurgic gods.
Creative Writing is
calendar poetry—
a broken pick-up truck
rusting in autumn weeds,
next to an empty barn.

CHAPTER SEVEN

You know this is the last chapter
when the waiter brings you the bill—
"the Last Judgment" in Spanish slang.
And it is not just for this life.
It's for all the lives you've charged up
while slumming around with bodies
to make sense in dual worlds.
Now comes the obscure reckoning:
what you're good at no longer counts,
what you're not is everything.
No one act or thing can redeem
another act or thing; each one
is inviolable and alone
and will not stand for anything.
I'm told that if you can stand it,
you're finally free to go beyond
the restaurant's revolving doors—
if you've enough left for a cab,
or can make your way in the night
to the home you once had uptown.

AMIGOS

Christ! cross off
the Mexican cantina
above the old port's
antiqued cobbled streets.
This is not Santa Fe.
The mechanical chips
in industrial cheese
insult Creation--
vinegar offered
instead of water for thirst.

LONGFELLOW SQUARE

Smaller than my cabin,
this apartment is
contractable to one.
With fewer books,
fewer beds,
the walls contain me.
Each illness
has subtracted
the self from me.
No work to clock,
no mate to attend,
I sit and stare
at time thickening
in rivered ice.
Now I know why
the old men
in Longfellow Square
sit to watch
the swifter traffic pass.

MUNJOY HILL

Transplanted to Portland
where the clouds are low, close,
and held part of the sea,
I walk the streets in search
of words lighting on things.
I come upon a weed
flowering in a ditch.
Even a dull raw weed
in summer can flower—
or, even a flower
at times must be a weed.

THE SEAGULL

Seagulls are glad that humans are such slobs;
they hawk the littered red brick and cobbled streets,
beneath the low clouds and above the billowy trash
of Starbucks napkins and tumbling paper cups
or toddler-dropped french fries and red pizza crust.
They easily rise to the sky or descend to the street.
Perhaps, *mon cher Baudelaire*, the albatross
is not our *semblable* emblem anymore.
Now the seagull is our *prince de nuées*,
at once the sky's clochard and the streets' *habitué*.

OCTOBER

I sit out in mid October
on the still open sunlit deck
of Brian Boru's Irish pub
with a view of the River Fore.
I promise not to write about
New England's colored autumn leaves,
the orange pumpkins and russet mums.
I know all that is just nature
left over from Wordsworth and Keats.
Besides, what I see are two trees
more rust colored than maple red;
the rest are a malingering green
in this oil and coal man-made heat,
I sip my Geary's Autumn Ale
and wait for Greenland's ice to slide.

CONGRESS STREET, NOVEMBER

Aslant the tilted autumn light,
I'm hard inclined to walk uphill,
although the sun disturbs my sight
and makes my shadow longer still—

a kind of comment on my life
and its karmic trail behind me—
longer for its transcendent strife
escaping mere humanity.

A schlepper of Lebensmittel,
without a pension or used car,
age has left me very little,
except the cut heart and the scar.

Food and shadow I drag uphill,
with past present in mind's remorse
for chance and choice, fate and free will—
the light and rocks in water's course.

IN GRITTY MCDUFF'S PUB

Over the copper-topped bar,
I write in my black notebook—
Letts of London with Cross pen.
A glass of Chilean red,
instead of Gritty's bitter,
is set out to my right hand
in an old fool's fondest hope
it's hops that bloat his belly.
The barmaid's cleavage on tap
suckles my bard's second sight.
Do breasts make us drink more beer—
the St. Pauli girl with jugs?
What am I thinking about?
I need here to look beyond
her cleavage or Maine's rock ledge
in this deep-harbored old port
of call to the Maritimes:
Yarmouth, Halifax, St. John's,
or else I'll become like
that squat boat out the window—
DiMillo's Floating Restaurant—
sated and going nowhere.

LUNCH AT DIMILLO'S FLOATING RESTAURANT

Margaret Mary O'Leary,
my grandmother, left Ireland
to die young in cold Chicago,
dead in her twenties from TB.
I am my own diaspora,
scattered odd personalities
that tried to find soil and take root
in Chicago, L.A., New York,
Dublin, Cambridge, and Toronto,
the Hamptons, Crestone, Bern, Zurich,
Honolulu, San Francisco,
Crestone again, then Santa Fe,
and now finally Portland, Maine.
In each I tried to be someone
who might be native to the place,
though my accent was never tuned
to Irish or American
but both at once yet out of place.
It's best I live in a tourist town
where I can pass as passing through,
which, if you think of it, I am.

AN ECONOMY OF SCALE

The random undulations of large flakes and wind,
the forming crystals' slumming attractions to dirt,
the updrafts and coyish hesitations of their fall,
the unnumbered cumulative facticity
of millions of interlocked flakes aloft in air,
the invisible droplets becoming cascades
of abundant redundancies of dense clouds let go
in the downsizing of the sky into the streets
for an instant slop the tires spit back to the curbs.

AT THE END OF THE FERRY PIER

The squawk of the seagull, the apocalyptic scream
of St. John the Divine's Cathedral Close peacocks
carve out of a vast space the bird's short territory.
Shall I squawk or scream at old age's solitude
that strikes a chiseled final self out of the time
near death? Once on the deck of Cisco's summer house,
overlooking the park of the Côtes du Luberon,
I heard the nightingale's operatic aria,
sung alone in the forest and dark stellar night,
while the nested territorial birds all slept.
In old age I finally caught up with Keats's ode—
counter-jumper Keats, once dismissed as "cockney school"
by the snobbish Tory rag, *Blackwood's Magazine*.
Keats in his calm London suburban neighborhood
never may have seen through his lowly chemist's trade
half the things he got from reading Chapman's Homer.
Did nightingales sing on Hampstead Heath, did skylarks
startle the sky in his brief tubercular walks?
I guess I will settle for the small nightingale
and go out singing, and not waste time in trite lament,
or hanging around, like the beaked scavenger seagull,
for odd scraps from someone else's intended dawn.

MARCH STREETS

Dirty snow is piled by the curb—
coffee grounds from winter's frothy
sipped cappuccino of clean snow.
Cigarette butts are frozen in
the black pock-marked ice like so much
rubble in a glacial moraine.
My street is winter's cadaver,
neither living nor buried yet—
no future for any of this.
March will melt before the tourists
return, dropping their midden trash.
Schooners will be back at the dock;
enormous cruise ships will again
seem tall apartment buildings parked
a few steps from Commercial Street.
Retired seniors will walk in groups,
taking digital photos of
the Old Port's 19th century
red brick buildings and cobbled streets.
I've made it through Portland's winter.
Soon I'll give strangers directions,
as if I were native to the place,
and not myself piled melting snow.

MARCH RAIN

The March rain makes no sound,
until the tin gutters
around my roof obstruct
its atmospheric fall.
My life would be silent—
emptiness without form,
movement unmarked by time—
if no struck obstructions
were set to sound me out.

ST. CUTHBERT'S DAY

The grit of sand on bricks,
the trash of a season
sticking to dirty snow,

within an icy rain,
I track the detritus
of winter in the streets.

Thirty-four years ago
in a bright crocused March,
you—Ah!, old man, move on!

MIDDLE STREET

The sound of steel turning on streets,
then the metal percussive crack
of the skate board on the side walk.
Three bored young males in baggy shorts,
waiting for their war, take their turns
in testing edges and seeking risks.
Walls, stairs, street traffic barricades
turn the city into a beach
of gnarly curbs and concrete waves.
Inside semen and big cities,
there are just too many, many
useless, unmatable young males.
What do you do with so many
when their numbers are set for death,
like mating spirals of May flies?
When we have peace, they will join up
in homicidal teenage gangs.
They declare their own private wars,
and don't wait for our Presidents
to send them off to die somewhere
where their deaths can be put to use
in protecting the price of gas
or keeping the air force aflame.
Tibetans once tried to ship kids
off to monasteries at ten,
to get them out of sex and death.
But now that Tibet is China,

Tibetan kids are fighting back.
Romantic poets got it wrong.
Nature is not nice or noble,
or even pretty any more.
There has to be a better way
than this street fight of sex and death.
No wonder Buddha wanted out
And got off in meditation.

THE AMERICAN ECONOMY

The handmaidens of despair meet in their webs of intrigue.
Scissor ears with iPods clip the news and BlackBerries
go picking themselves through the NSA traces
but the server is down and the market is skittish
as unemployment goes south and futures sell short.
The beggars of description roll the credits in the streets.

CONGRESS STREET, APRIL

I walk Portland's streets,
voicelessly at work,
editing the world,
correcting grammar,
chastising smokers,
erasing tatoos
telling Maine's obese
they should be ashamed
to be as fat as
rural Southerners
who skipped evolution,
health and nutrition.
These Yankee obese
drive electric carts
because if they tried
to walk they'd break hips
and legs and would slump
into adipose
sidewalk deposits.
Smoking and drinking,
eating disorders--
Ice Age Goddesses,
anorexic teens—
body tattooing,
inserting metal
and crystal meth
and wild molecules:
these folks write themselves
off on their bodies.

HURRICANE BILL

My ice white hair is thinning out,
the Greenland ice sheet is as well.
We both seem an age put to rout
as things around us start to swell.

The implications of an act
are now the clutter of an age.
The air itself begins to wrack
revenge on land with sea-filled rage.

Earth has gone from riches to rags:
clear cut forests, coal blackened air,
islands of floating plastic bags
only tectonics could repair.

A Hyperborean event,
for which I am situated
confirms "nature is never spent,"
and never manipulated.

CASCO BAY

As the sun is high
In this cleared blue sky

It's hard not to feel
That the Earth is real

Everything is so
More just than so so

It is not our birth
That binds us to Earth

Who can remember
Soul's flame or ember

Or breath's foreign gasp
The sting of time's asp

Some recall our fall
Most nothing at all

And of our first weeks
Behind bars' first peeks

We know the room's light
has sounds of dark fright

We have to be taught
Life's is and its ought

These islands at sea
Mark reality

As something between
Surface and unseen

At the bottom we
Look up in a sea

Of infinite stars
More real than ours

Midnights in Crestone
I'd listen alone

To the Pleiades
The seven ladies

Now six from the blast
That turned us outcast

Startled and hurled
To this island world

When I heard that song
How could I belong

But with sea and sky
Living I might try.

CARLETON STREET HAIKU

Portland, I've come round:
cherry blossoms are in bloom.
How many springs left?

MAINE MALL

On the empty spaces of the vast parking lot,
the seagulls ignore the neatly white painted lines
and, legs folded up, lie flat on the black asphalt.
They seem to have their own normative crowding rules
and keep a wary distance from one another.
Seagulls are proud opportunists not sheepish pigeons.
It is nine, but the stores do not open till ten.
I learn this is when the seniors mass in the mall.
Couples take their brisk cardiovascular walk
down the full length of the quiet uncrowded halls.
They don't hold hands as they have their hearts on their
minds
and walk intently as if death really means it.
At the tables of the Food Court the men gather
to read the morning paper or play cards in fours.
No worry beads are fingered here, no watch is kept
on the sunlit life of the young passing them by.
This is not Crete where the aged are, with the trees
and tavernas, architecture to the filled square.
The cleansed piped-in music has not yet been turned on,
and the silence seems as unnatural as the plants.
The air is conditioned, the sunlight is corraled
and only to be found grazing in square skylights
not really needed to illuminate the halls
forming the Swiss cross of this twined Galleria.
The aluminum curtains in front of the stores
begin to lift in their own artificial tide,

and as they do the seniors are lifted with them.
It is now time for the untrophied wives to shop.
Outside, the seagulls give over the parking lot
and drift under the low seaborne cumulus clouds.
They will return when the shoppers of fast take-out
become the next flooding tide of dropped Food Court scraps.

IN RIRA'S IRISH PUB, I

This pint glass
has no fondling curves,
no female waist
to welcome fingers
treasuring the heft,
the partner's pas de deux
lift into the amber light,
the foam-kissed lips
of body raised in offering--
a memory lifted out
of bog-darkened water
around the brain's recesses--
curved, *curtós*, cur-tossed,
the Tollund bog man,
a scapegoated redeemer of past time
with cap and cord still around his neck;
its straight lines are abstracted thought,
a merely linear act of insertion,
without all the crevices
for touch and lips
in a gift of tongues.
Consider the squat
conventional Portland ferries
through this other glass.
Also uncurved,
unstreamlined,
built to be slow

as the lift of a pint,
they look made out of Leggos,
squared for easy adhesions,
to hold and to last.
And why not?
Paper clips and staples—
practical objects that serve to link
readings' odds and ends—
are still around with Kindles.
I take note of things
that have been around
as long as I have.

IN RIRA'S IRISH PUB, II

Four ferry boats moored in a row,
yellow and white with red top trim;
black cormorants skim the surface,
then dive in search of food gulls miss,
what I with sinking words would do.
(brim-wylm onfeng   hilde rinc)
The cormorant's dive leaves a ring,
as I do on this *Geary's* glass.
Old words when lifted to the tongue
also ring from their touch with things--
Sutton Hoo burials of boats
in earth with Saxon treasures now
ferried across surfaces of
cheap American floating trash.

PENCIL SKETCH

Three Dollar Dewey's with raw-wintered floors,
thirty-six handled taps of beer and ale,
cruddy recorded heavy metal rock,
baskets of popcorn, talkative strangers
in Maine pub conversations at the bar.
No sullen drunks here scrying their iced glass,
no one set to go off into a rage,
no vintage wines and cuisine—standard fare,
and brews a buck less than Irish RiRa's.

IN RIRA'S IRISH PUB
WITH HORACE'S SECOND ODE

Dactyls and trochees once trampled the Earth,
scrolls of twisted history kept time.
Next came barbarians with torched hands
reading with flames.

Old as I am, now I'm allowed
things occupations scorn or ignore—
Latin studied willingly and Horace
read in pubs.

Portland's Irish pubs serve me well--
cornered away from TV and bar,
tapping inspiration with stout microbrews
tongues will tell.

Humans see movies in twenty four
frames per second, but birds can see
two hundred and forty per second
gestures of time.

Colors they see amazingly in 4D—
dogs can see only two, but we see three.
Dark and light, then colors, but what
do birds see?

Poets see the present as futures' past:
watching the valleys fill, mountains
scab over with cabins, trees flushed out,
flooded by grass

Towers fall, sea coasts rise,
tectonic plates rattle around,
crashing and breaking continents apart—
Atlantis and Mu.

Tidal breathing of the sun and seas,
multiple times are on all at once:
Abaris and Amergin, Taliesin and Yeats—
swallows in flight.

PUB POEM: TO HORACE'S FIFTH ODE IN GRITTY MACDUFF'S

Who now lingers spent in his long moment,
Pyrrha, in that pink orchid-gated cave
Of coral and shell and a sea gods' odors?
If he's inside, entranced, he cannot see
Neptune's jealous tides rising at his back
To fill you and flush one more out to sea.

PUB POEM: TO HORACE'S ELEVENTH ODE BY WAY OF HAFEZ

At seventy, are you still trying to outguess the gods,
lifting the lid, prying the jar, sniffing around for clues,

to see on which overheated star they're cooking up stews
for catastrophes of fire or ice, earthquake, volcanoes,

or Deucalion's floods twice up to Jove's Olympian toes,
and droughts from Phaeton driving the car while DWI.

Are you still striving to be some Druid bard who can scry
the future through writing chicken scratch runes on bleak gray stones?

You're no Chaldee reading stars, or African tossing bones,
no Sibyl giving god head and coming out of her mouth,

no twice dead Indian swami from the treacherous South,
passing the basket around while his kid picks their pockets.

Are you really profound, with your eyes rolled in their sockets?
You'll trip and break your neck long before the apocalypse

is reflected in the sibylline slobber on your lips.
We're March wind's tumble weeded souls caught in Earth's barbed wire,

So, carpe diem!, Thompson, and let the wind be higher
than you are with its dried seeds of spring and reviving fire.

TO HORACE'S ODE XIII

You, my Janus-faced Janice,
goddess of love's doorways,
you who tell of old lovers,
praising Robin's brigand grace,
Robert's courtly mannered take,
Frank's great committed heart—
fate has left me off the scroll.

I see their history in your eyes.
You are what you've become
alone in warm nights with them.
Supple and well-spent, a glove
fittingly bent to muscle and bone,
holding the form that's been put in.
Me? A swallow whose nest is gone.

Why call for second rounds, add
another verse to the ended song?
I've still the faults I had at first,
weathered more by a life in words,
not solid like Frank's science,
Zen like Robin's impermanence,
Nietzschean like Robert's madness.

I am like old cracked jade
Chinese scholars keep at hand,
touching the stone while they brush
landscapes disappearing in the mist.
I'm now the god above the door,
holding life open in the frame,
words fading as we both pass through.

PUB POEM TO HORACE, LIBER II, XI

Pakistan's crumbling, Afghanistan's next,
Somali pirates attack our ships,
and Ill is making our President vexed,
while GM is nothing but pink slips,

Brother Chet, the Empire's down
like Ill's fizzled rocket into the sea;
at our age of seventy and eighty,
we're hooked off stage to call in the clown.

Obama is young, at the top of his game,
he can rule the skies in Air Force One;
the Empire's his to slaughter or tame,
and civilize Goth, Vandal, and Hun.

The borders where we need to keep watch
are slack bodies where muscles are few,
and couvade pregnancies bloat out our paunch,
as our breath grows short and hard to renew.

So forget the news it's time to break
out the cellar and drink up the rack:
of Hundred year-old Orkney Scotch,
Chateau d'Yquem and Champagne Cognac!

Yes, I know it's bad for cirrohtic livers,
Rosacea red nose and liver spot,
but before fate stands and delivers,
bring up all of the best that you've got.

You've made your money, good elder brother,
although we both have lost our good looks,
and if money is only CDs and paper,
so are all my published books!

PUB POEM IN BULL FEENEY'S
TO HORACE, BOOK III, ODE XVI

Laurance, now that your soul's on high,
well-deserving in an Elysian field,
I think of you and your Maecenan yield,
of Bandusian spring and "cabin in the sky."

Both now are in a Zen priest's ply,
one hand clapping, the other grasping,
encircling all in the square root of pi—
emptiness, it seems, is rather filling.

Bene est, cui deus obtulit,
parca quod satis est manu—
Hard-up for rent, I'm still at it,
since poets lack the Zen of Voodoo.

Portland has more shepherds than flock
of sheep with monkish heads full shorn
in Crestone's deserts of conglomerate rock
staring with blank faces of the unborn.

Here the springs are barreled tubs
of fine New England microbrews
on tap in Portland's Irish pubs
where portraits of poets observe the pews.

I lift my pint to you, my Mentor,
remembering your profile in the glass
high atop Rockefeller Center,
watching sun and snow flurries pass.

I saw you'd been a three-pronged fork--
Marcus Aurelius and Magnifico Lorenzo,
and I his poet-friend Poliziano,
with you in Rome, Florence, and New York.

If past lives are just ways we can boast,
to portray the One in the Many,
then accept without believing my toast
as a gift in return for your money.

Next life, let's trade marbles in play,
and let me be generous among men;
I too will give Maecenan millions away,
but never a cent for Japanese Zen!

AFTER CATULLUS II

Little sparrow
in the furrow
how my girl teases
as she pleases
with tidbits,
peeps and twits
sweet painfully
you and me.

With single finger,
the morsels linger.
I wish I could speak
with finger to beak
in soft feathered fuzz
just as she does.

AFTER CATULLUS XXXII

I'm hard to love you, my soft Angeline,
my scented garden, my privates' desmene.
Come now, it's high noon, the sun too is hot.
My door is open; it's only a trot.
I need your nine ways of sucking me clean
Dry with your foamed mouth, entranced sibylline.
Come, and come again, as you can just by
drinking me up with your daimonic cry.
Come quick, I am seized in priapic throes,
pointing skyward in my pole-tented clothes.

AFTER CATULLUS 51,
WHICH ITSELF IS AFTER SAPPHO 128

Lindisfarne-in-Manhattan, 1977

That one seems to me to be like like a god,
or a scientific law transcending gods;
seated opposite to me he leans toward you.
Listening only

to you, with a smile he disposseses me
of my senses possessed by you,
and when I look at you together I'm lost
without sight or speech.

The ringing in my ears, my demented eyes
go black with the stopped blood in my breathless chest;
my seizure is final as your sweet laughter
terrorizes me.

A vision of your sandals under his bed,
and I am the city this god has laid waste,
and you the garland laurel for the strong arms
of him, my good friend.

AFTER CATULLUS LXXXV

I adore and abhor my adoring and abhorring of her.
Why I don't know; I'm wracked and mad to do so.

FREE STREET

A parking cop marks the tires
with chalk before he writes a ticket
for the over-stayed residents of time.
I marked out Portland with poems
as I prepared to move on in.
Impermanence is good for Buddhists.
We Judeo-Christians need to nail
down time to God, after all we
crucified Christ in Jerusalem
and Christianity in Rome.

BACK COVE

I admit I have run aground.
No creative tide lifts my mind.
Like this cove, my thoughts are stuck in
sea-abandoned back water mud
where seagulls search for stranded life—
accountants who reckon the cost
of things exposed flat on ledgers
long after any uplifting act.
No Creator God or Gnostic
Archon with a devlish twinkle,
designing a platypus, squid,
or mud-dipped hippopotamus
ever ran aground—amuck,
maybe, with flea and stink beetle
whose ass in air seems up to give
creationists the third finger.
When a god is not inspired,
he naps while imps and devils play.
When a poet has run out of
high thoughts for floods of poetry,
he needs to muck about knee deep
in what the cleared mud exposes.

ANOTHER KIND OF MADELEINE

The smell of the neighbors' cooked food
in the stained linoleum halls—
a memory of running down
the hall of another transient
apartment building smelling of
hamburgers fried in bacon grease.
I was emptying the day's trash
to be helpful so that I could
stay home and not have to go back
to the feared military school
where I had lived, summers as well,
for two years from seven to eight.
As I opened the door, my Dad
in rage slapped me hard in the face—
terrified that we'd be thrown out
for having kids that made kid sounds
as they ran down the rug-less hall.
I look down at the coffee stains,
unmopped for months, smell the fried meat,
and try to pass without a sound.

THE CONFERENCE OF CROWS

Always at sunset out my high window
I see hundreds of black crows congregate
on the top branches of winter's stripped trees.
Yesterday they perched on the metal roof
of the apartment house across from me.
Many hurry as if they will be late.
The orange light of the low winter sun
seems to call them like a visual *Adhan*.
They hurry to find their place and then turn
and become quiet as they watch the sun.
In Zurich I used to watch a black bird
alone at sunset on top one high tree
sing out in his enjoyment of the light.
Birds can see four dimensions of color;
dogs can see two and we humans see three,
so I like to imagine that the sky
shifts for them in ultraviolet bands
of audibly bright spectral auric light.
When the sun has set and the sky turns gray,
the service ends and all the birds depart.

MID-WINTER MOOD

A low cold cloud bank obstructed my walk.
There would be no sunset, no open sky.
Intentions countermanded, I went home
to draw the curtains and turn on the lights.
This winter darkness feels catastrophic.
Solon told Plato those near the sea drowned
in tides, those on mountains died from the sun.
Sometimes it just doesn't pay to be there
wherever you are trying to be safe.

WINTER HAIKU

Gulls fly in snowfall.
Snowflakes do not stick to them,
sliding off feathers.

Planes do not fly well
in sleet or clouds holding snow.
Metal attracts ice.

This short northern day
cannot soak up the long night;
darkness blots light out.

Moonlight in the ice
on the gutters of my roof.
The stars can't do that.

ICICLES

Upon the decorated cornices
of Portland's brick Edwardian buildings,
daggers and spears of icicles depend.
If you come under their dentellated lace,
the bright entrancing crystals can become
a heaving form bringing down on you
a portcullis of points impaling skulls
in a wet shift from perfect frozen skies.
Your soul learned this before with a comet
that crossed your path with head of light and tail
of dry and frozen ice. Better to give
in touch with winter this new sunlit ice
a wide berth to bear in on a yogic
death and avoid that attractive beauty.

MAINE LANDSCAPE

Life is lust—better said
in German than English.
The women imagined
as nudes became naked.
The prizes I hoped for
were awarded by minds
huddling all together
in a herd ass-ended
into the real wind.
Time to go it alone.
I hear the hollow sound
of the ice underneath.
The path behind is cracked;
no point in turning back.
If I turn back, what then?
Here there is the beauty
of this snow-covered lake,
this Zen calligraphy
of the stark cracking ice,
a *kinhin* for my steps.
The white snow, the blue sky,
all this is as perfect
as I need it to be.

THE MODERN POET

The tossed away newspapers turn
in the autumn wind, one lifted
on to the point of its corner.
The old pathetic fallacy
would say it is dancing,
but I know better. Instead I
think of turning gyres announcing
the birth of some rough beast slouching
toward Bethlehem to be born,
for we are moderns after all,
alluding to one another,
and not to some animistic
raw primitive sense of nature.
I mark how the wind turns the page,
but will not say it reads out loud;
instead I'll think of how old news
decays into its elements
and not think of elementals
tearing human nature apart,
breaking down surface histories
into recycled pulp and slop,
since we now do that for ourselves.

NANCY GRAYSON'S BOOKSTORE

Nancy's used bookstore is closing.
It was the best bookshop in town—
prints and photos of old Portland
on the walls, classical music
always playing as she sipped tea,
by her collection of small busts
of great composers and authors
that seemed to chide the larger statue
of Henry Wadsworth Longfellow
you could see through the store window
overlooking Longfellow Square.
The bookstore down in the Old Port
died a year or so ago. I bought
a novel by Wendell Berry there
and the owner talked to me
eagerly about Wendell's work.
Now there are only four bookstores
left in Portland, three used, one new.
The store in Monument Square sells
magazines, cards, travel novels,
and commercial fiction. It feels
more like an airport concession
than a place to linger and talk
to the owner about new books.
The used bookstore on Munjoy Hill
is more for collectors of rare,
costly antiquarian books,

but *The Green Hand* with its life-size
stuffed seven foot Yeti that greets
us at the door leads us into
an Old Curiosity Shoppe
with a museum of "Weird Life"
at the back that can speak volumes
about the fossils of old books.
Russ's *Yes* used bookstore across
from Starbucks at High and Congress
is like a rent-controlled pre-war,
dark, downtown New York apartment
cluttered with the secret thoughts
of someone proud of depression
as a badge of adjustment to
to universal suffering.
With high piles of books on the floor
that block the shelves, you can't see what
Russ has behind, so you end up
not able to buy anything.
Used bookstores are cemeteries—
books weathered tombstones of authors
once famous but now forgotten:
Thomas Costain, Eugene Field,
Charles Morgan, Philip Wylie.
And, of course, I find myself here
in an unread first edition—
hardbound from 1981.

But now it is not just authors
that are becoming fading ghosts,
but bookstores and books themselves.
e-books will ephemeralize literature and history,
until some solar maximum
wipes out iPads and ATMs

and we are left in the clutter
of our own silent devices
to start from scratch on rocks again.
I think the Great Pyramid must
be a CD for which we've lost
the reader; or perhaps the gods
gave up and took it back with them
to the stars in Orion's Belt.

SEASONAL CHANGE

A thick fog with rain drops bubble
wraps my brick apartment building.
The cold radiators trouble
me with their silent annoying

insistence it's still late summer.
After all, it's officially fall--
October and not September.
My landlord is aloof and tall,

and certainly Republican,
so he votes to keep the past in
office for as long as he can
keep progressives in the trash bin

of history along with Marx
and the Socialist Welfare State.
Fear not the treason of the clerks,
rather the Fed and interest rate.

The Market's apotheosis
has given us a new Greek god
who with Chicago Boys' gnosis
can hide uneven with odd

to prove that greed adds up to good,
except that in my neighborhood,
you still can freeze your low rent ass
off in the cold warfare of class.

RADIATORS

That hot steamed old metallic smell
of radiators cranked open
to the sound of rust-rattled pipes
and a snake-like sibilant hiss
of the basement's underworld
broke up my fall afternoon nap
into memories between me
and the underrealm of the dead.
I recalled the smell of wet wool—
of plaid winter coats left to dry
after playing out in the snow
on the park set into Drexel
Boulevard and Ingelside Av.

It was Chicago in the war
and my uncles sent me V-mail
full of bravery and good cheer
and trivial family things—
never a word about Hitler.
Uncle Eddie came back, but Jack,
a conscientious objector,
died when the ramp of his landing
craft opened up to the bullets
on Normandy's Omaha Beach.
My mother said he never had
to kill anyone, so he died
without disgrace, a sacrifice
to family, flag, and country,

innocent of the guilt that would
have killed him had he made it home.
It was Uncle Jack that gave me
my blue and black plaid winter coat
for Christmas. This was long before
Goretex and light weight ski parkas,
when winter held the smell of wet wool,
dripping on hot radiators.

THE STRIKING SOUND
OF RAINDROPS

When it's raining and you don't
have to take the required
cardiovascular walk,
the inwardness of your small rooms
opens its possibilities to you.
The sound of the rain on tin gutters
is comforting—a zendo filled
with incense and intimacies of space.
Things begin to seem
more than they have to be.
Those who messed up their lives
sit with satorial pretentiousness
because they have nowhere now
as some new kind of take-out place.
The guy next to you is divorced
and like Buddha a deadbeat Dad,
the woman on the other side
is Catholic, had an abortion,
and was dumped anyway.
Some tried to get work
but were rejected more than once,
so sangha now is their only hope.
The Ab.D as an incomplete
has put too much into his robes
to leave now that he's been given a title
and a Zen bib to put his hands behind.

The roshi exists on a higher plane
and sits in more costly robes
and imported Japanese accessories.
He surveys them all, one-pointed
on the next student he will seduce.
They all want to be like him.
Where was I? Listening
to the *monono aware* of the rain,
thinking when I shouldn't,
with an I that is not really there,
trading satori for a play with words,
feeling my uninstitutionalized room
fill with the sense of presence,
glad to be a writer alone
with the Western lineage of words
and not a monk weighed down
with emptiness enclosed in robes.

GERONTION

e-mail in the mornings,
start clicking with the *Times*,
checking the *Guardian*,
Le Monde Diplomatique,
Al Jazeera, Juan Cole,
the NZZ—that's Zed—
sluming in the tabloids
of the *Huffington Post*,
I surf the web and world,
to find if it's still there.
No earthquake yet has hit
Tokyo or L.A.,
no Greenland ice sheet yet
has slipped into the sea,
flooding the undergrounds
of London and New York.
The day is still within
an era and not yet
beginning another.
There still is time to take
a long walk to the sea,
watch the yellow ferries
cross the suburban bay
carrying day shoppers
with wire grocery carts
filled with toilet paper.
The cruise ships and schooners

are not yet docked apart;
this in-between season
hangs around like the trash
the gulls and cats live by.

I walk out to the end
of the pier, note the sea,
then walk the slow hill home.
Unable to afford
a restaurant or pub,
I cook my own quick meal—
something in-between lunch
and a censored dinner
with all the salt removed--
take a nap, make white tea,
ride nowhere for a while
on my exercise bike,
read methodically
through nuanced passages
of school boy languages
not fully understood.
I nod off like Homer,
wake absurdly refreshed
to toss and turn all night,
get up and start again,
minding the gap between
back then and not quite yet.

CLYTAEMNESTRA

Looking down at the water in the bath,
she remembered how her water first broke,
and silently released her ten years' wrath,
with the battle ax hidden in her cloak.

The hero split from crown to collar bone
two-faced slid into the perfumed water,
silently relaxed, never having known
his wet death was revenge for her daughter.

Then as an afterthought, she unmanned him.
With the rage of ten years waiting relieved,
she remembered, humming a bridal hymn,
the jasmine night Iphigeneia was conceived.

ON READING
THE PENGUIN BOOK OF ENGLISH VERSE
ON MY IPAD AND EXERCISE BIKE

For the twentieth century, the Irish
have possession for more times than you would think.
Possessed by archaic words that like stones
in the soiled richness of their dark speech
obstructing progress and breaking plows,
they know the blessed curse of not forgetting.
Funerals are their real celebration
of life. No one can be praised until dead,
lest the *Sidhe* and old gods kidnap the child.
They prefer mad to sane, drunk to sober,
celebrating the rural storied object
over the City's speed-drugged bank routine.
But when the Irish get into money,
they become caricatures of excess—
as we see in the scat left on the land
by the Irish banks and Celtic Tiger.
As your common drunk is a failed mystic,
your entrepreneur is a Brit manqué.
But where are the Irish women poets?
Is it always to be Heaney and Longley,
Kinsella, Carson, Mahon and Muldoon,
With the token colleen ni Cuhuilleanáin?
We Yanks have produced Brigid's lineage.
Why should only the men be vatic bards?
Where are the wild sybils the gods ride hard?

Are women too burdened holding men up?
My father was a drunk, preferred life in bars,
ordering a round to buy the respect,
he couldn't earn at home with food and rent,
and when Mom nagged him, slugged her in the mouth.
Once she'd had an infected tooth removed—
her blood gushed on the red mahogany
where she'd set out the pile of bills unpaid
because of what he'd spent on getting drunk.
He slugged her in a rage; a jet of blood
shot out from her wound onto the table
and carpet she had worked herself to buy,
lace curtain Irish that she was, but disowned
for marrying a divorced Protestant—
a boom-time salesman and Depression drunk.
His karmic reward that cold winter was
pneumonia and the pain of sclerderma.
The war ended, we moved from Chicago
to LA , a city without neighbors
or Catholic relatives to define us.
Dad's sclerderma-clawed hands hurt too much
to hit Mom, so there was an untruced peace,
and he moved out to an old veterans' home.
The dream-drunk Irish recoil from dull life—
the old cult of heads cut off from bodies—
and Dad's inability with money
got hold of me as I would rather write

than work for millions, speculate in land,
or be tenured as an academic.
Reading this book through shows me how I am
not truly English or American.
Americans—Beat or Black Mountain—are
more poets of the eye than of the ear,
formal verse is too rooted and contained;
they love Williams' open typography,
Ginsberg's flashing Gay exhibitionism,
Ashbery's overheard conversations,
randomized lines, and *The New Yorker's* chic
preference for the prosaic poem.
No wonder I end up in Portland, Maine,
in between one West Coast and another.

APARTMENT LIVING

At midnight my neighbor starts
to play his music loud—
siege engines to my soul.
Two by fours and sheet rock,
and nothing in between,
is what my landlord calls
a wall. My neighbor likes
country western disco rock—
some seventies medley,
Nashville homogenized—
faux country truck drivers'
Interstate levelings,
not Appalachian folk.
I'm transported to see
big buckled cowboys, gals
with piled peroxide hair
and Dolly Parton tits
square dance in petticoated
short skirts and cowgirl hats.
True faked Amerika,
this long-necked Bud's for you!
David Byrne, how did I
get here? Did I forget
to mention Memphis—or
diss Palin's NRA?
I thought Maine would be safe.
New Hampshire's not Vermont,

nor Maine Massachusetts.
Now wherever I go—
Crestone or Santa Fe--
I cannot find the ground
that fits me like a sole.
This fake music tells me
I need to move again.
There's only one place left
as far as I can see.

LENI RIEFENSTAHL AND THE TRIUMPH OF THE SUPER BOWL

When commercials trump the program,
and the two teams are much the same,
it is time to transcend the game
to worship Money's hologram.

The interference of the light,
with a second radiant source
makes the object of brutish fight
pure praise of economic force.

What our culture is now about—
politics, sports, and TV spots—
is not what the fans think they shout,
but programmed minds for patriots.

THE NINETEEN-FIFTIES

Where did all my opinions go?
Once my day was completely filled
with judging everything I'd see.
Like rungs of a ladder that held
opposite sides apart I'd know
how to rank things to define me:
cars, of course, flavors of ice cream,
movie stars with pointed tities,
and my favorite football team.
Now I care less about the show,
the text-messaging in the dark,
twittering with celebrities.
If life's a loud carnival land,
with sexual rides that rise and swell,
mixing visual fun with fright,
then Samsara's a Disneyland,
entertainment's a kind of hell,
and Nirvana is out of sight.

LONGFELLOW SQUARE

You can see the city change here
in quickened cinematic time.
On the south side of Congress Street,
blear-eyed uncentered drunks gyrate
in front of the jack-off parlor
and beg for busfare and dollars—
even begging costs have gone up.
Under the attended cherry trees,
the old and street regulars meet.
Above in his classical chair,
Longfellow sits looking beyond
dollars and cents, counting Greek feet.
Five new upmarket restaurants
have bet they'll drive the lowlife out.
Nancy's used bookstore is to be
turned into a Literary Bar,
but the porno store is still there,
renting DVDs for old men
too homely to date and get laid.
The louche transsexual gay bar
is flaunting itself in sad drag
eyed customers who smoke outside.
The music club, the sushi bar,
the upscale Parisian bistro
will win the day as the cheap rent
leases run out and the rates go up.
Money will drive down-market sex

out, just as the sleek Cruise ships
filled with retired Kansas couples
matched in baby blue leisure suits
and jogging shoes with Velcro straps
drove the Old Port's sailors and whores
from the gas lit and cobbled streets.
The antique is too good to waste
on aged hippies, the homeless,
and crystal meth country folk.
Longfellow above the street life
sits this dithyrambic one out.

AN URBAN ANCHORITE

I no longer write in cultural hubs
like Manhattan, Berne, Zurich, or Paris.
I tried writing in Portland's Irish pubs,
but my doctor's warning and prognosis

shifted me from microbrews to white teas
in silent laptop desk establishments
where no one bothers to offend or please.
No longer able to afford the rents

in rich cities with *caché* and *élan*,
where my literary career once whirled,
like Prospero exiled from proud Milan,
I have learned to live in liminal worlds

far from the Corso's evening parade
of men with their costly sweaters neck tied
and girls with breasts half covered, half displayed,
hoping by fashion to be verified.

Now I have taken to my yogic cave,
where alone with *Daimon*, angel, and jinn—
and sometimes on the Shakti's Tantric wave—
I write seized in Daimonic transmission.

If that way solitary madness lies,
in the other way vision ossifies.

THE WESTERN PROMENADE

The black Labrador dog poops
on the grass by the sidewalk.
The alabaster coated
master stoops to pick it up.
With plastic meticulous
bagged hand he bends to collect
lab assistantly each
dark but scientific turd.
I think my consort angel
often feels the same dismay
at my dark excreted thoughts.

THE COFFEE CANTATA:
DIE UNERTRÄGLICHE SEHNSUCHT

Certain moments of beauty that take you
by surprise so brutally uncalled for
embarrass you with tears because they reach
behind the Roman stage for street living
and recall the primal hurt, the raw shock
of incarnation and so become torn
satyrs like Marsyas exposed to light.
Why did Bach have to sneak into of all
places the comic *Coffee Cantata*—
before Mozart's *Nozze di Figaro*—
the sublime trio with so trite a text
as *Die Katze läst das Mausen nicht*?
But isn't that just how it is with life,
when all that you are is interrupted
in its casual business of lying
by the unbearable flayed longing
of the life left behind you in the stars?

POETRY

One day it just stopped:
as if God had turned
a dripping faucet off.
Perhaps He was right:
enough water had drowned
in words' detergent froth.
Now what? As I looked
into the mirror it seemed
tired of reflecting me.
What was it then
that turned to face
the morning, whose streams
of light moved me
along anonymously
intent on everything
in the created streets?
Adam's naming of things,
and not Eve's apple
was the Fall. The snake?
He had only one letter
to write endlessly
in the unlettered grass.

NEUROSCIENCE I

The act of intentional will comes late—
after the neurons demonstrate

each voluntary intended act
is a facet of an unseen tesseract.

Consciousness is an afterthought—
the bill for the meal you've already bought.

The waves of the sea
do not touch the sky.
There is more to me
than meets the I.

NEUROSCIENCE II

My windows frost over
in winter's ice-bound night.
I shift my focus to
the intermediate
realm of ferns and snowflakes,
just as at midnight I
shift my mind away
from the perceived world
of physical objects
to daimon, angel, djinn.
If all this is brain-based—
mere hypnagogic trance—
then think of it an art
much more interactive
than gallery displays,
operas, or concerts.
You believe whatever
you want. I desire
whatever I believe.

REINCARNATION AND THE AKASHIC RECORD

Out of the night my mind comes back
with knowledge of lost worlds and times
before birth and death edited
one long story into chapters

of wars, cruelty, and murders,
mercy and redemption merited
through suffering, remorse for crimes,
as soul puts body on the rack—

a Russian novel complexly
woven with so many subplots,
we forget the first characters
we left behind about to make

a great and terrible mistake:
a senate of conspirators,
a conjured jealousy that rots
Othello's mind rationally,

or Anna who chose one love
over another and then kills
herself crossed on two steel rails
leading to yet another life

where she becomes Karenin's wife,
for when one decision entails
another's life, our trouble coils
and the snake entangles the dove.

LINDISFARNE FELLOWS CONFERENCE, 2011

I.

When we pass on,
think only this of us:
we lived alert
to the rapids and breaks
of the heart's cascade -
its loud blood
percusive music
in our ears,
as we encountered rocks,
marking our passage
in a broken open time.

II.

My friends are dying
fast ahead of me.
Ideas we held
start to come apart.

A tidal island
lent its ancient name
and shared its spirit
in refracted time.

When the tide withdraws
and the road is dry,
perhaps we shall cross
times to try again.

ZUCCOTTI PARK, 10/31/2011

This tented settlement
is indeed an occupation—
a job for the unemployed,
a new inner vocation:
Abraham called out of Ur
to live a life in tents,
waiting for the Elamites
to set the Sumerian script,
"Lament for the Destruction of Ur."
The suspendered men in suits
work behind the walls
of the cop-protected Street.
Ananké has cornered the dollar
and shorted human time
in favor of the high rollers
you can sense out at sea.

EXTRAORDINARY RENDITION

Intentionally at dream-break,
the eyes focus on the strange room.
The shock of not knowing who one
is does not compute space or time.
With no memories of the place,
no ready-made self springs to mind.
Terrorred disorientation
claws the papered walls to tear off
the outer package, to get at
an objective world, something known.
Like an act of grace, memory
begins a collection in time
to provide a me for what I see
out of my mind and world.
Twenty four hours of air travel
and bardo transit terminals
have given me an overture
of death and life in overtime.
Trams, trains, escalators, airplanes,
tunnels, shuttles, small planes, taxis,
and a friend's car have got me here
from Switzerland to Arkansas
in a day without sleep or a sense
of real travel under stars,
of passage through narrative time—
King Melchior on a camel.
The terrorist is arrested

in Hamburg, hooded, drugged, and shipped
bound to Diego Garcia.
He wakes to find his body gone:
nothing to see, nothing to hear,
then a scream of sirens, a blast
of loud Heavy Metal music,
breaking the rhythm of his heart,
as he finds his body turned on,
appliant to their electric
wired crib of scientific
"aggressive interrogation."

BLUE MOON, AUGUST 31, 2012

Two times this August the moon has been full.
Our solar calendars are too numskull.
Goddesses are not law-bound married wives.
You lead more rich and complicated lives.

Our solar calendars are too numskull—
a mine propped up with a weak timbered stull.
Men cannot corral clouds or fence the sky,
and wives aren't branded cows to scarify.

Goddesses are not law-bound married wives.
You are Space where your vast power derives.
You are the Earth under no man's command,
and your love is not water to be dammed.

You lead more rich and complicated lives.
Through your turning the sun daily arrives.
I am your moon, your secret tidal pull.
Two times this August the moon has been full.

ANATAMAN

The stars I see are no longer there,
behind their light speed images.
The life I see in memory's reflection
is also no longer there.
I have little future and no real past.
My vanishing present is suspended
between two non-existent poles.
This I of mine is like a rainbow:
it disappears when I get too close.

PHILIP K. DICK SPEAKS
FROM THE BEYOND

It has come to pass
that Google Glass
can now read minds
and if it finds
your thoughts unpatriotic
or radically Quixotic,
then "they who should not be named"
do not become inflamed,
but with a software poke,
you suffer a cerebral stroke.

SMARTPHONES

The living dead walk Portland's streets,
eyes and opposable thumbs held
to a tool whose history repeats
medieval cities magoneled,

and free prokaryotic cells
tumbling in the Archaean sea,
tasting the clear bubbly micelles
turning an I into a We,

as what was once just two or three
creatures moving near each other
became locked in a unity
for ATP under cover.

Cells no longer replicated
each other ad infinitum
but lost one half and duplicated
in an open continuum.

Such goings on produced a self,
with an apparent conscious mind,
as fairy, gnome, imp, sprite, and elf
emerged completely undesigned.

Now the wave of self starts to ebb,
its permeable membrane closed
and locked within a world wide web
where a free mind is not disposed

as each brain becomes a synapse
that need only signal and fire
while the glials with other Apps
rule from levels that are higher.

The transfixed synapse need not know,
since this new planetary mind
keeps each brain locked within the show,
making each one all of a kind.

So it was once that walled towns fell,
and castled barons appended
to crowns that had the magonel
and the Middle Ages ended.

As once upon a time the cell
enclosed what came first to eat it,
and spirochete turned organelle,
now history seems to repeat it,

as mindless brains don't need to think,
and fucking couples text their friends,
more drawn to the Web's need to link
than whatever mere sex intends.

Now sex is gone, death must be next,
as smartphones can transmogrify
time with an App for turning text
into a me without an I.

COMING OUT OF THE ER
IN DAMARISCOTTA

Tumbling syllables
of Maine sunlight
manicly lift my spirits
to silence spoken in loud
clapping
of my one-handed
mechanical valve—
my atrial fibrillating
over-Joyed heart.
I am so glad to be
out of love
and into the time
I'm really in.
As it's past,
I can really ask:
"What the hell was that?"

Now a chipper geezer
with smart walking stick
I'll twirl and whistle
a new tune
in the right time and key,
smile and tip
my Fred Astaire straw hat
at the friendly Maine young girls,
and they, as they always do,
will smile back
and think: "What a sweet old man!"
for now I am
off the rack.

THE WESTERN PROMENADE:
Instructions to My Daughter for My Last Rights

The right not to have the last rites.
As a Catholic altar boy,
carrying a candelabrum
by the coffin on its way out
to the black Cadillac hearse parked
at the foot of the steps in front
of Immaculate Conception,
I began to hate the display
of candle and smoking incense,
the insipid hymns that at least
helped rid me of my awkwardness
since nobody knew what to make
of death and none of that priestcraft
seemed to help anybody but
the nuns and veiled old ladies
who came to church every day.
So I want none of that clerical
fraud for my own heretic's end.
No funerals, memorials,
not even a fine Irish wake.
Those who want to remember me,
tell them to go and read my books,
so they all don't go out of print.
John Synge wrote that for Aran
Islanders "going west" meant death—
disappearing in the vast sea,
dying from disease or famine,

or leaving for America.
So here I am at the West End
of Portland on the Promenade.
In front of me is all the West:
in the distance, snow-capped mountains,
the River Fore, the Interstate,
airport, oil tanks, a low rent mall,
brick offices and parking lots.
When Greenland melts into the sea,
this estuary of glacial mud
will again become a great fjord.
Now there is nothing Romantic
about this economically
developed commercial valley,
so you could put my ashes here
instead of Monhegan Island
or distant Katahdin Mountain.
With Maine Medical to my right,
the cemetery to my left,
it has its own finality.
The Eastern promenade does have
a better view of the islands,
the sea and ships in Casco Bay,
but I lived here on the West End.
So, without ceremony, come—
Evan and Andrew if they can—
on a day very much like this,

bright and clear to the White Mountains,
and when the sun is in the West,
put my ashes here in the ground,
lift a glass to the sunlit West,
then pour a cup of single malt
over them and place a good stone,
common and unmonumental,
to mark the place for you alone.

William Irwin Thompson

ABOUT THE AUTHOR

William Irwin Thompson (1938–2020) was born in Chicago, but moved to Southern California in 1945, where he graduated from Los Angeles High School in 1957 and Pomona College in 1962. He received a Woodrow Wilson Fellowship to study at Cornell in 1962 and a Woodrow Wilson Dissertation Fellowship to do his doctoral research in Dublin in 1964. He received his doctorate from Cornell in 1966 and published his first book, *The Imagination of an Insurrection: Dublin, Easter 1916 in 1967*. In 1972, his second book *At the Edge of History* was a finalist for the National Book Award. In 1986 he won the Oslo International Poetry Festival Award for his novel, *Islands Out of Time*.

Thompson taught at Cornell, MIT, and York University in Toronto. He forged an interdisciplinary career; and studied anthropology, philosophy, and literature at Pomona, and literature and cultural history at Cornell. He has served as visiting professor of religion at Syracuse University (1973), visiting professor of Celtic Studies at St. Michael's College, the University of Toronto (1984), visiting professor of political science at the University of Hawaii at Manoa (1985), Rockefeller Scholar at the California Institute of Integral Studies in San Francisco (1992-1995), and Lindisfarne Scholar-in-Residence at the Cathedral of St. John the Divine in New York in the autumn of each year from 1992 to 1996. In 1995 he designed an evolution of consciousness curriculum for the Ross School in East Hampton, New York and served as a Founding Mentor. Thompson founded the Lindisfarne Association in 1972 and served as its Director until 1997. William Irwin Thompson continued to devote himself to writing essays and poetry and was a contributor to the *Wild River Review* in retirement.